UNDERSTANDING IMMIGRATION LAW

How to Enter, Work and Live in the United States

UNDERSTANDING IMMIGRATION LAW

How to Enter, Work and Live in the United States

Nancy-Jo Merritt

Chelsea House Publishers

Philadelphia

First printed in hardback edition in 1997 by Chelsea House Publishers.

This book is published in order to provide accurate information regarding immigration. It is sold with the understanding that, while the author is an attorney, the author and the publisher are not engaged in providing legal opinions or other professional services. Do not use this book as a substitute for obtaining qualified legal or professional help.

1 3 5 7 9 8 6 4 2

Library of Congress Cataloging-in-Publication Data

Merrit, Nancy-Jo, 1942-
    Layman's law guides. Understanding immigration law / by Nancy-Jo Merritt.
        p.cm.
Includes index.
    ISBN 0-7910-4444-0 (hc)
    1. Emigration and immigration law—United States—Popular works.
I.Title.
    KF4819.3.M47 1997
    342.73'082—dc21   96-37516
                                                    CIP

This book is published in order to provide accurate information regarding immigration. It is sold with the understanding that, while the author is an attorney, the author and the publisher are not engaged in providing legal opinions or other professional services. **Do not** use this book as a substitute for obtaining qualified legal or other professional help.

Instead of writing combinations of the pronouns "he" and "she" as he or she, he/she, s/he, we have elected to use the word "he" uniformly throughout this book when identifying a person. The use of "he" is not meant to be offensive, but is written for the sake of convenience and consistency.

ACKNOWLEGEMENTS

I owe particular thanks to my partner Lenni Benson who corrected mistakes and reminded me of information I had left out, to Brian Burke who gracefully eliminated the thousands of unnecessary commas I had obsessively placed in the text, and to Charles Kuck for patiently reading the early drafts. Thanks also for the encouragement and assistance I received from my other partners in the Immigration Department of Bryan Cave, Roxana Bacon and Angelo Paparelli.

Finally, I could not have completed this book without the patient instruction in word processing I received from Susan Brester, a super-star secretary who clearly does not need to worry that I will ever be able to function without her.

Nancy-Jo Merritt

TABLE OF CONTENTS

••

INTRODUCTION 1

CHAPTER ONE
CITIZENSHIP: ARE YOU A CITIZEN? 4

Claim to Derivative Citizenship 4
  U.S. Citizen Parent(s) 4
  Naturalized Parent(s) 6
  Marriage 6
Proof of Citizenship 7
Loss of Citizenship 8

CHAPTER TWO
THE VISA SYSTEM: WHO IS INVITED TO THE U.S.? 10

Non-Immigrant Visa Categories: Alphabet Soup 10
  "B" Temporary Visitor, for Business or Tourism 11
  "E-1" Treaty Trader 12
  "E-2" Treaty Investor 13
  "F-1" Academic Student 14
  "H-1A" Registered Nurse 16
  "H-1B" Specialty Occupation 16
  "H-3" Trainee 18
  "J-1" Exchange Visitor 19
  "K" Fiance or Fiancee of U.S. Citizen 19
  "L-1" Intracompany Transferee 20
  "M-1" Non-Academic Student 21
  "R-1" Religious Worker 22
The Immigrant Visa: Lawful Permanent Resident Status 22
  Family-Sponsored Immigration 23
    Immediate Relatives: Spouses, Parents
      and Children of U.S. Citizens 23
    First Preference: Unmarried Sons
      and Daughters of U.S. Citizens 27
    Second Preference A: Spouses and Minor Children
      of Permanent Residents 27
    Second Preference B: Adult Unmarried Sons
      and Daughters of Permanent Residents 28
    Third Preference: Married Sons
      and Daughters of U.S. Citizens 28
    Fourth Preference: Brothers and Sisters of U.S. Citizens 28
  Employment-based Immigration 28
    First Preference (Priority Workers) 29
      1A: Extraordinary Ability 29
      1B: Outstanding Professors and Researchers 29

1C: Multinational Executives and Managers 30
Second Preference 30
  2A: Advanced Degrees 30
  2B: Exceptional Ability 30
Third Preference 31
  3A: Professionals 31
  3B: Skilled Workers 31
  3C: Other Workers 31
Fourth Preference: Religious Workers 32
Fifth Preference: Investors 32
Asylees and Refugees 33
  Refugees 33
  Asylees 34
Miscellaneous Categories 35
  Displaced Tibetans 35
  Diversity and Transitional Programs 35
  Hong Kong Provisions 36
  Schedule A 37
  Registry 37
  Widows/Widowers 39

CHAPTER THREE
SEEKING ADMISSION: CAN YOU COME IN? 40

Entry 40
Where Do You Apply to Enter? 43
  The U.S. Consulate 44
    Non-immigrant Visa Applications 44
    Immigrant Visa Applications 45
  Port of Entry 46
Adjustment of Status 47
Visa Status 48
U.S. Laws 49
Employment Authorization 50
Summary 51

CHAPTER FOUR
THE "GREEN CARD": WHAT DOES IT MEAN? 52

Lawful Permanent Residence 52
Loss of Permanent Resident Status 54
  Abandonment 54
  Deportation and Exclusion 57
  Recission 58
Summary 59

CHAPTER FIVE
DEPORTATION: CAN YOU BE SENT HOME? 60

Who Can Be Deported? 60
Grounds of Deportation 61
Relief from Deportation 64
  Expungement/Pardon 64
  Voluntary Departure 66
  Suspension of Deportation 67
  Registry 69
  Adjustment of Status 69
  Waiver of Deportation 70
  Asylum and Withholding of Deportation 71
  Deferred Action 73
  Private Legislation 74
Deportation Hearings 74
Consequences of Deportation 77

CHAPTER SIX
NATURALIZATION: BECOMING A CITIZEN 79

Who Can Apply? 79
When Do You Apply? 79
How Do You Apply? 80
Requirements For Naturalization 80
  Literacy in the English Language 81
  Knowledge of History 81
  Residence Requirement 82
  Moral Character 83
Barriers to Naturalization 83
The Oath of Allegiance 84
Consequences of Citizenship 85
Denaturalization 86

CONCLUSION 88

INTRODUCTION

The immigration and nationality laws of the United States are complicated, but with a little effort you can determine your rights and figure out the best course of action to reach your immigration goals. The most important rule is that you must follow the statutes (written laws) which tell you what you must do to enter the United States or to become a permanent resident or a citizen. The immigration and nationality laws are found in the United States Code. Ask your librarian to show you volume 8 of the U.S. Code. The Immigration and Nationality Act begins with section 1101 of volume 8.

Almost as important as the statute are the regulations which explain how the statute is to be implemented by the Immigration and Naturalization Service (the "INS"). The immigration regulations are found in a separate book, volume 8 of the Code of Federal Regulations. (These volumes go out of date quickly, so ask the librarian to help you find the current regulations.)

You must be honest, do what the law requires, and be very careful and attentive to detail if you are filling out any forms.

Finally, the Constitution of the United States contains provisions that may affect your rights. Many of its provisions apply to "all persons," which includes non-citizens, even if they are not in the country legally.

The statute and the regulations are lengthy, but remember that they contain the actual law that governs your status if you are not a citizen of the United States. The Constitution also contains important protections which ensure that you are treated fairly under the law. If you wish to be successful in making your way through the maze of the immigration laws of the United States, you must be honest, do what the law requires, and be very careful and attentive to detail if you are filling out any forms. Most of the INS forms you will need are available free of charge from your local INS office. (A list of INS offices is included in appendix A.) If you have trouble locating a form, you may wish to call the United States Government Printing Office for assistance. Check the "blue pages" of your phone book for the federal government toll free information number, listed under "United States—General Services Administration."

The best way to think of U.S. immigration law is that it is designed to ensure that everyone who comes here is within those groups that the Congress has decided are needed to improve the United States, such as those bringing special expertise or skill, or who fulfill some national goal, such as reunification of families. In addition, the immigration laws reflect a clear congressional goal to keep out, or "exclude," undesirable persons such as convicted criminals, terrorists, and anyone who tries to enter the United States fraudulently.

An understanding of the immigration and nationality laws of the United States requires an understanding of the terms "citizen" and "alien."

An understanding of the immigration and nationality laws of the United States requires an understanding of the terms "citizen" and "alien." The Fourteenth Amendment of the U.S. Constitution defines citizens as "all persons born or naturalized in the United States and subject to the jurisdiction thereof." An "alien" is any person who is not a citizen of the United States.

There are three kinds of aliens. Non-citizens who entered illegally or who have violated the

2

terms of their visa status are referred to as "unlawful" or "unauthorized" aliens. Persons who entered on temporary visas for limited time periods are "non-immigrants." Finally, aliens who have received permission to live and work permanently in the United States are called "resident aliens," "immigrants," "permanent residents," or may be referred to as having a "green card."

Now let's take a closer look at the law.

CHAPTER ONE
CITIZENSHIP: ARE YOU A CITIZEN?

The Constitution, the supreme law of the United States, says that all persons born in the United States (which generally speaking also includes birth in Puerto Rico, Guam, the Virgin Islands, and the Northern Mariana Islands) are U.S. citizens. There is an exception for children of foreign diplomats. Because diplomats are not subject to the jurisdiction of the U.S., their children, even if born inside the United States, will not be citizens. Otherwise, the nationality or the status of the parents does not affect the acquisition of citizenship of a child born inside the United States. If you are born in the United States, you are entitled to have a U.S. passport, and you do not have to meet any residency requirements in order to keep your citizenship.

Some people may be surprised to discover that they have a claim to U.S. citizenship.

Claim to Derivative Citizenship

Some people may be surprised to discover that they have a claim to U.S. citizenship, even though they were born outside the United States. Although citizenship is acquired most commonly by birth in the United States, there are three ways a person born abroad can claim U.S. citizenship.

U.S. Citizen Parent(s)

An individual born outside the U.S. may be a citizen if one or both parents were citizens at the time of his birth.

Citizenship obtained in this manner is called "derivative" because it "derives" from the citizenship of your parents. If you want to demonstrate a claim to derivative citizenship based upon the U.S. citizenship of a parent, two things are necessary. First, one or both of your parents must be citizens at the time of your birth. Second, certain residency and retention requirements must be met by both the parent and child. Charts which show the requirements based upon your date of birth are found in Appendix B. The law is different depending on when you were born, and there are different rules for the transmission of citizenship to illegitimate children.

Four questions must be answered to determine whether you can claim derivative citizenship based on the citizenship status of your parent.

Four questions must be answered to determine whether you can claim derivative citizenship based on the citizenship status of your parent:

- When were you born?

- How long did your parent(s) live in the U.S. before your birth?

- Were your parents legally married?

- Are any of the "retention" requirements applicable?

(During some years derivative citizens had to live in the U.S. for certain amounts of time before a certain age in order to "retain" their citizenship; these are the retention requirements.)

It may be necessary for you to be a bit of a detective to determine whether you have a valid claim, and the expertise of a specialist in immigration law may be required to deal with some of the little known provisions that may affect your case. For example, an ancestor may have been naturalized under a law that entitles active duty veterans of the U.S. Military to citizenship status without fulfilling the usual preliminary requirement of first becoming a lawful permanent resident and then waiting for five years. Or, if the citizen ancestor had to have lived in the U.S. for ten years, five of them after the age of sixteen, you will need to locate documents, such as old school records, military records, or U.S. census records, to prove that your relative met the residence requirement.

Naturalized Parent(s)

An individual who was a lawful permanent resident of the U.S. at the time his parents were naturalized may be a citizen.

An individual who was a lawful permanent resident of the U.S. at the time his parents were naturalized may be a citizen. One or both of the parents must have been naturalized, and there are residence requirements for the child claiming status and for the naturalized parent. The child must have been a permanent resident before the naturalization of the parent, but the qualifying age of the child varies, depending on the year of birth, as you can see in the chart of Appendix B.

There are special rules for adopted children. After October 10, 1978, an adopted child of naturalized parents may derive citizenship only if he was under the age of eighteen and living with the adoptive parents at the time of naturalization of the parents and if the adoption was completed before the child reached the age of sixteen.

Marriage

Before September 22, 1922, a woman became

a citizen automatically upon marrying a male U.S. citizen. Becoming a citizen in this manner was available only to women; no application had to be filed, and there was no naturalization procedure. Women who married non-citizens also obtained the benefit of automatic citizenship if their husbands became naturalized citizens after the marriage.

This route to citizenship ended in September of 1922 and is no longer available. Marriage to a U.S. citizen now only entitles the husband or wife to apply for lawful permanent resident status, and it is not automatic.

Proof of Citizenship

If you were born in the United States, your birth certificate is the best documentation of your U.S. citizenship. It should be a government-issued document, not a certificate issued by a hospital. If you only have a hospital certificate, contact your birth state to see if you can get an official birth certificate. Persons born outside the United States may have a record of registration with a U.S. Consulate.

Your birth certificate is the best documentation of your U.S. citizenship.

If you are claiming citizenship derivitively, you may make an application for a U.S. passport with the Department of State on the form DSP-11. You must apply in person at the local passport office. You can find the address in your phone book in the United States Government listings under "passports." Alternatively, you can file the INS form N-600 with the Immigration and Naturalization Service for a Certificate of Citizenship. The preferable method is to apply directly for a passport, as it will be issued much more rapidly and can be used for travel.

There are many unusual and little-known ways to become a citizen. If any of your direct ancestors have lived in the United States or were married to a citizen, you should explore the possibility that you already may be a citizen.

Loss of Citizenship

Once you are a citizen of the United States, either by birth or naturalization, you can lose your citizenship only by voluntarily taking actions, called "expatriating" acts, with the intention of giving up United States nationality. If you have no intention to give up your citizenship, you cannot lose it.

If you have no intention to give up your citizenship, you cannot lose it.

The law lists seven specific acts which, if performed voluntarily with the intention to relinquish United States nationality, will result in loss of your citizenship:

- Obtaining naturalization in a foreign country after the age of eighteen.

- Taking an oath of allegiance to a foreign country after the age of eighteen.

- Serving in the armed forces of a foreign country during hostilities against the United States, or serving at any time in foreign armed forces as a commissioned or non-commissioned officer.

- Serving as an official of a foreign government after the age of eighteen if you are also a national of that country or if you took an oath of allegiance required by the employment.

- Formally renouncing citizenship before a U.S. diplomatic or consular officer outside the United States.

- Formally renouncing citizenship in writing while inside the United States during wartime, if the Attorney General consents.

- Committing any act of treason, or attempting to overthrow the U.S. government by force, or bearing arms against the government.

If you give up or lose your United States citizenship, you become an alien subject to U.S. immigration laws should you later decide you would again like to live and work in the United States.

CHAPTER TWO
THE VISA SYSTEM: WHO IS INVITED TO THE UNITED STATES?

A visa is a stamp placed in your passport by an official of the State Department, usually a consular officer, outside the U.S. The visa stamp is not a guarantee of entry, as your actual physical entry is governed by the INS, which is not part of the State Department, but is a subdivision of the Department of Justice. However, the first step is a visit to a U.S. consulate to obtain a visa stamp, unless you are a citizen of a country that has an agreement with the United States which waives the visa requirement. Citizens of a number of countries, including Italy, France, Germany, and the United Kingdom, may visit the United States for up to ninety days without first obtaining a visa, provided that they have a return ticket home, and are travelling to the United States for a temporary visit as a tourist or business visitor in the B-1 or B-2 category.The visa system of the United States is divided into two parts: one for immigrants and another for non-immigrants.

It is important for you to speak with a consular visa officer or with an attorney who specializes in immigration law.

Non-Immigrant Visa Categories: Alphabet Soup

Non-immigrant visas are temporary, time-limited, and with one exception, are available to unlimited numbers of applicants. Non-immigrant visas are each identified by a letter of the alphabet, and each type has its own distinct requirements. It is important to be familiar with the rules for your visa category, because activities which are not appropriate for your visa status may mean an early departure from the United States.

The following descriptions are of the most commonly used types of nonimmigrant visas. These brief summaries may not give you enough information about the requirements of a particular visa to allow you to know if you are eligible, or, you may be eligible for one of the visa categories not generally available to the public and not included in this book. It is important for you to speak with a consular visa officer or with an attorney who specializes in immigration law before making any important decisions.

"B" Temporary Visitor, for Business or Tourism

This is the visa most often used to enter the United States. It allows you to enter the U.S. temporarily, usually for six months or less, to conduct business (category B-1), or to travel for pleasure (category B-2). A "B" visa does not allow you to accept employment of any kind, although if you are coming to engage in business, you may consult with business associates, attend conferences, and do other things which benefit your foreign employer. You may not receive U.S.-source payment for services in the United States.

To be eligible for a "B" visa, you must have a residence in a foreign country which you do not intend to abandon.

To be eligible for a "B" visa, you must have a residence in a foreign country which you do not intend to abandon, and you must intend to remain in the United States only for a specific temporary period. You make application at the U.S. Consulate nearest your foreign residence, on Department of State form OF 156.

"E-1" Treaty Trader

This visa is available only to nationals of countries which have treaties of friendship, commerce and navigation with the United States. You should check with the U.S. Consulate nearest your foreign residence to see if your country of citizenship has such a treaty. An applicant for an E-1 visa must be coming to the United States to carry on trade principally (more than 51% of the company's total volume of trade) between the U.S. and the foreign country of which he is a national. There is no requirement that you have an unabandoned foreign residence, and treaty aliens may spend long periods of time in the U.S., so long as the trade continues.

The E-1 visa is available only to nationals of countries which have treaties with the U.S.

Spouse and children of treaty traders also may have E-1 visas, but their employment is not authorized. The company itself may be organized in the U.S., but the majority (more than 50%) ownership of the company must be by nationals of the treaty country. Permanent residents of the United States may only be minority owners, even though they still hold citizenship in the treaty country.

The E-1 visa also is available to managerial or executive employees with skills essential to the operation of the company. In order to qualify for an E-1 visa, however, an employee must be a national of the treaty country.

The standard non-immigrant visa application, the OF 156, must be filed with the nearest U.S. Consulate. If you are in the U.S., you may be able to apply for a change of status to E-1, if you are still in a valid status and have not engaged in unauthorized employment.

The Consulates in treaty countries have instructions and questionnaire-type forms to assist applicants for E visas. The application process can be document-intensive and can require several weeks of processing time at busy consulates.

The period of validity of an E-1 or E-2 visa stamp varies from country to country, but E visa holders will be admitted to the U.S. for cne year at the time of each entry. If you are irside the United States at the expiration of the one year period of admission, you must apply for an extension to stay, before the expiration date.

"E-2" Treaty Investor

This visa should not be confused with the immigrant investor visa (also known as the "employment creation" visa); the "Treaty Investor" visa is a non-immigrant visa and does not confer lawful permanent resident status.

The treaty investor visa is available to persons coming to the U.S. to develop and direct the operations of a business in which they have invested, or are in the process of investing, a substantial amount of capital. As with the treaty trader category, spouses and children may accompany the principal alien to the U.S. The company may also obtain visas for employees with essential skills or who are executives or managers.

The treaty investor visa is available to persons coming to the U.S. to develop a business investment.

Treaty investor visas are available only when more than fifty per cent of the business is owned by nationals of the treaty country, who may not be permanent residents of the United States.

The most commonly asked question about this visa is how much money is a "substantial" investment. There is no simple answer, but a general rule is that the amount of capital invested in the business must constitute more than half the value of the business. If it is a brand new business, the amount of money invested must be more than half the amount needed to start such a business. If you are applying for an E-2 visa and you are also the owner of the business, you must also show the consular officer that the money invested is your own and that you are personally "at risk" for the failure of the business. For example, if the investment capital is the result of a bank loan in which the only security for the loan is the assets of the business, the loaned funds may not be included as part of your investment for purposes of demonstrating that you have invested a substantial amount.

The amount of capital invested must constitute more than half the value of the business.

In addition, the business must generate more income than the amount necessary to support the investor and his family at a marginal level. "Marginality" is not defined, but the usual way to avoid the problem is to show the consular officer that the investor has other sources of income than the U.S. business, that the business will employ persons other than the investor's family, or that the business is now generating or is likely to generate substantial income.

You may apply for a treaty investor visa at the U.S. Consulate nearest your foreign residence on the form OF 156 and the Consulate's Treaty Visa Questionnaire.

"F-1" Academic Student

Applicants for student visas must demonstrate an unabandoned foreign residence and that they are coming to the U.S. to pursue a full-time course of study at an academic institution. Spouses and children of the student will be allowed to accompany the student and will be granted F-2 status. Neither F-1 nor F-2 status includes employment authorization, although students may accept on-campus employment of less than 20 hours per week, and after completion of one academic year of study, students may apply for a limited employment authorization from the INS.

Applicants for student visas must have plans to pursue a full-time course of study.

A full-time course of study is at least 12 hours per term or, in the case of graduate study, the amount certified by the institution as constituting a full course of study for graduate students.

Students must first obtain the form I-20AB from the institution, demonstrating that the student has been admitted by the school. The consular officer will place the F-1 stamp in the passport and designate the length of stay as "D/S," which stands for Duration of Status, the period of time necessary to complete the course of study plus one additional year to engage in any approved work experience (practical training).

At the time of entry, foreign students will be issued the INS form I-20ID in addition to the I-94. The student must keep the I-20ID, which will contain the student's admission number, with him at all times.

Prospective students who enter the United States with a B visa must apply for change of status to F-1 in order to remain in the country as a student. You should be aware that ninety percent of all requests for change of status to F-1 are denied. It is preferable to obtain the student visa prior to entering the U.S., or to tell the consul of your plans to become a student and look for a school. The consul will note that you are a prospective student on your passport next to the B visa Stamp. With this notation, you should have no problem when applying for change of status.

"H-1A" Registered Nurse

Employers who wish to hire professional practicing registered nurses must first file a Health Care Facility Attestation with the Department of Labor (the DOL). This is a document in which the employer attests that it has been unable to recruit sufficient nurses in the United States and that it is engaged in the active recruitment, promotion, and training of U.S. nurses. The employer then must file a visa petition with the INS on the INS forms I-129 and Supplement H. All non-immigrant visa petitions which are filed with the INS are filed at one of its four regional service centers. The address of the service centers can be found in Appendix A.

The prospective nurse employee must be licensed to practice in the country of his nursing education.

The prospective nurse employee must be licensed to practice nursing in the country of his nursing education, and must either be licensed in the U.S. in the state of employment, or must have a temporary license and take and pass the first available licensure exam. The law providing for this visa category is scheduled to expire September 1, 1995, unless extended by Congress.

"H-1B" Specialty Occupation

In order to apply for this visa, you must have

a job offer and your prospective employer must have done two things: it must first have filed a Labor Condition Attestation (LCA) with the DOL, and have received a notice of acceptance; it next must file a Petition to Employ Temporary Worker or Trainee on INS form I-129 and Supplement H at the INS service center in the region where the employment will take place. The INS will send the approval notice to the Consulate, and then you may apply for your non-immigrant H-1B visa. If you are in the U.S. in a valid status, you may request that your status be changed to H-1B.

In order to apply for an H-1B visa, you must have a job offer.

The LCA requirement is similar to the H-1A attestation that employers of foreign nurses must file. The LCA requires the employer to attest that hiring the alien employee will not have an adverse impact on the wages or working conditions of similarly situated U.S. workers. The process also requires that the LCA be available for public inspection and that notice of the prospective hire of the alien worker and the salary to be paid be posted. The employer must also agree to pay the return travel costs if the employee is fired.

The H-1B visa is available to persons who have at least a bachelor's degree, who are being hired to work in an occupation which requires such a degree and, if state licensure is required to practice in the occupation, are licensed. It may be possible to qualify for an H-1B visa without a university degree, if you can demonstrate that you have degree-equivalent experience, such as progressively increasing positions of responsibility in the occupation over a lengthy period of years. The U.S. employment must always be a position that requires a degree.

There is a limit of 65,000 H-1B visas that can be issued in any fiscal year (October 1 to September 30). The H-1B visa can be extended for a total stay of six years, but it allows you to work only for the petitioning employer. Authorization to work for another employer is allowed only after the new employer has received approval of the LCA and its H-1B petition for your services.

Graduates of foreign medical schools may not have H-1B petitions filed on their behalf unless they are coming to teach or conduct research, or have passed the FLEX exam (given by the Federation of State Medical Boards) and are competent in oral and written English. (Canadian medical schools are not considered "foreign medical schools" for this purpose.)

"H-3" Trainee

This visa is for persons coming to the United States to receive training. The company proposing to offer training must first file and obtain approval of a petition on INS form I-129 and Supplement H. The approval notice is sent to the U.S. consulate nearest your foreign residence, where you apply on the standard non-immigrant visa application form OF 156.

This is a very restrictive visa category, and the company must demonstrate that its training program is actually a training program and not being used for productive work or on-the-job training for a future visa. The training program may not exceed two years.

"J-1" Exchange Visitor

The specific attributes of "J" visas are complex and restrictive. The programs which allow for the entrance of exchange visitors are subject to the administration of the United States Information Agency (USIA). If you are considering applying for an exchange visitor visa, you should investigate the program thoroughly or consult an immigration lawyer. Exchange visitor subcategories include students, research scholars, trainees, professors, teachers, and other miscellaneous international visitors. All "J" visitors must be sponsored by an exchange visitor program, and many programs require that the "J" visa holder return to his country of residence for two years following completion of his stay in the United States.

Foreign medical graduates may enter the U.S. to obtain graduate medical training only with a "J" visa, under the sponsorship of the Educational Commission for Foreign Medical Graduates (ECFMG), and will be subject to the requirement to return to their country of residence for two years following the completion of the exchange program.

Foreign medical graduates may enter the U.S. to obtain graduate medical training only with a "J" visa.

"K" Fiance or Fiancee of U.S. Citizen

This visa is for those persons coming to the U.S. to marry a U.S. Citizen within 90 days. The prospective U.S. citizen spouse must have filed and obtained approval of a Petition for Alien Fiance(e), INS form I-129F in advance of the visa application. The petition is filed with the local INS regional service center. The INS sends the notice of approval to the U.S. Consulate nearest the fiance's residence. Because the alien is coming to the U.S. to take up permanent resident status after marriage, this visa is processed similarly to an immigrant visa, and requires some of the same preliminary steps, such as a medical exam. The process may take six to nine months.

The petitioning citizen must demonstrate that the couple actually have met in person, and that the marriage will not be entered into merely as a convenience to obtain permanent resident status for the alien spouse. The marriage must take place within ninety days after entry. If it does not, the fiance must return home. A change of status to another category is not allowed.

As an alternative, you could marry abroad and your alien spouse could apply for a permanent resident visa at a U.S. consulate. This process will take approximately four to six months, although you should check with the local Consulate for more specific information about its processing times. There is a more detailed discussion of the permanent resident visa application process in Chapter Three.

"L-1" Intracompany Transferee

This visa is for employees of multi-national companies who are needed in the United States to work for the same employer (or its subsidiary or affiliate), as a manager, an executive, or in a position which requires the employee's specialized knowledge. The nationality of the company or the employee is not relevant to the visa, nor is the amount of the company's investment in the U.S. The company, or its subsidiary or affiliate, must have obtained approval of a Petition to

Employ Intracompany Transferee on INS form I-129 and Supplement L prior to the employee's application for the visa at a U.S. Consulate. The petition is filed with the INS regional service center for the area in which the employer is located.

Within the three year period prior to the company's filing the petition, the employee must have worked for the company outside the U.S. for at least one year, in the same type of capacity in which the employee will be working in the U.S. (i.e., as a manager, executive, or in an area requiring specialized knowledge). If the U.S. office has been established less than one year, the initial period of authorized stay in L-1 status will be only one year. Otherwise, the initial period of stay may be three years, with a total stay of seven years for managers and executives and five years for specialized knowledge employees.

The L-1 visa is for employees of multinational companies who are needed in the U.S.

Canadian citizens do not need a pre-approved petition, but may file the petition at a Canadian port of entry into the U.S. Canadian citizens do not need to visit a U.S. Consulate to obtain a visa stamp in their passport prior to entry.

"M-1" Non-Academic Student

This is similar to the F-1 student visa except that it is for students coming to the U.S. to attend a vocational school. The school issues the form I-20MN, and the student may be admitted for the period of time necessary to complete the course of study described on the I-20MN plus 30 days, or for one year, whichever is less. A period of practical training, not to exceed six months, may also be authorized.

"R-1" Religious Worker

This visa is for employees or members (for at least two years prior to entry) of religious denominations, who are coming to the U.S. to work as ministers or in a professional capacity for the denomination.

The application is made on INS form I-129, with Supplement R, and is filed at the nearest regional service center. The period of stay may not exceed five years.

The Immigrant Visa: Lawful Permanent Resident Status

An immigrant visa allows you to live and work permanently in the United States.

An immigrant visa allows you to live and work permanently in the United States, but such visas are available only in very limited numbers, pursuant to quota limitations decreed by Congress. The possessor of an immigrant visa is a "lawful permanent resident" (an LPR) and is allowed to work without restriction.

Permanent residents are issued a rose-colored Alien Registration Card, often referred to as a "green card," the color of the card many years ago. Once an LPR has lived in the U.S. for five years (three years if the resident is married to a U.S. citizen during that time period) after having obtained permanent resident status, he may apply to become a naturalized U.S. citizen. Obtaining an immigrant visa is the first step to citizenship.

The two most important ways to obtain an immigrant visa are through a family relationship or through employment.

Family-Sponsored Immigration

Visa petitions may be filed by family members for relatives in any of the six classes, or Preferences, described below. In most cases, the sponsoring relative files the INS form I-130 with the INS Regional Service Center nearest the residence of the sponsor. The addresses of the four regional service centers are found in appendix A.

Immediate Relatives: Spouses, Parents and Children of U.S. Citizens

United States citizens may file immigrant visa petitions for their legally-married husband or wife, parents (including step-parents if the marriage was entered into before the petitioning United States citizen reached the age of 18), and minor children (including step-children if the marriage to the alien spouse was entered into before the children reached the age of 18). A U.S. citizen son or daughter must be over the age of 21 to petition for a parent. There is no quota limitation on the number of immediate relatives who may be granted LPR status.

If your relative lives outside the United States, the immediate relative petition must be filed with the INS by the U.S. citizen by mail to the INS service center in the region where the U.S. citizen resides. Notice of approval of the petition is sent to the U.S. Consulate where the alien relative resides, and the immigrant visa process is completed at that Consulate (see Chapter Three). The alien relative will receive an immigrant visa stamp in his passport and may then enter the country as a lawful permanent resi-

Visa petitions may be filed by family members for relatives in any of the six classes.

dent. The Alien Registration Card will be mailed by the INS to the relative's address in the U.S.

If your relative is in the United States and entered in a legal manner by applying for admission at a port of entry, he may "adjust status" to LPR inside the U.S. instead of applying at a Consulate. In this situation, the petition of the U.S. citizen relative will be filed at the local district office of the INS, along with the alien relative's Application for Adjustment of Status on INS form I-485. This method is not available to all applicants for permanent residence. A list of the addresses of INS district offices is shown in Appendix A.

A U.S. citizen son or daughter must be over the age of 21 to petition for a parent.

The application process, whether at the consulate abroad or at an INS office in the United States, will be much the same. The alien relative must show that he does not fall within any of the grounds which would prevent entry. This requires a medical exam, proof of financial responsibility, and a criminal records check which is done by submitting a fingerprint card to the INS.

Immigrant visas are not derivatively available to the spouses or children of aliens who obtain LPR status as an immediate relative of a U.S. citizen. In other words, your spouse and children are not able to get an instant visa just because you are getting one. You will have to petition separately for your spouse and children.

Remember however, that if you are getting a visa because you are married to a U.S. citizen and your children have not yet reached 18 years of age, your spouse is a citizen step-parent who can file immediate relative petitions for your children as their immediate relative step-parent.

There are special anti-fraud rules that govern the grant of LPR status to spouses of U.S. citizens when the couple has been married less than two years. The anti-fraud rules were developed because the INS believed that many of the applications filed in this category were not based on "real" marriages. After trying many other methods, including asking the couple the colors of their toothbrushes or bathroom tile in separate interviews or sending investigators to their home to see if the closets contained clothes belonging to both persons, the current system was developed.

Special anti-fraud rules govern the grant of LPR status to spouses when the couple has been married less than two years.

Your alien spouse will first be granted Conditional Permanent Resident status which will expire two years after the date the status was granted. Then, within the 90 day period before the expiration date, the couple has to file a Joint Petition to Remove the Conditional Basis of Alien's Permanent Resident Status on INS form I-751. The petition is mailed to the INS regional service center for the area in which you live. You must show the INS that the marriage was not a sham or an accommodation, so that the alien spouse can complete the immigration process.

Here are a few tips on how to prove that your marriage is not a sham. Attach documents to the petition that show that you are still married, living together, and have the normal commingling of financial assets of a married couple, such as joint ownership of real estate or automobiles. Include bank account records, insurance forms showing beneficiary designation, family photos, and of course, the birth certificates of any children born of the marriage.

If the marriage has not lasted for the duration of this two year period, the alien spouse may file the I-751 with documentation to demonstrate that the marriage was entered into in good faith and not for the purpose of evading the immigration laws. The documentation should include the same records that would be submitted with the Joint Petition, and an explanation why the marriage is no longer viable, perhaps accompanied by letters from friends who can attest to the marriage having been genuine.

The requirement to file the I-751 jointly may also be waived if the alien spouse would suffer extreme hardship if he were to be deported, or if the United States citizen had subjected the alien spouse or child to extreme cruelty or physical abuse. The I-751 should be accompanied by documentation proving the hardship or the abuse. For example, if the reason for the waiver is abuse, the alien spouse might include police reports, medical records, or affidavits from friends or counselors.

The INS is concerned about the use of fraudulent marriages to circumvent the immigration laws.

The INS is concerned about the use of fraudulent marriages to circumvent the immigration laws, and thus there are specific grounds of exclusion and deportation for marriage fraud. Persons desperate to live in the United States often think of phony marriages as an easy route to permanent residence, perhaps after hearing from friends how easy it is or after watching movies such as "Green Card." DO NOT EVEN THINK OF IT. It is extremely foolish to consider a marriage of accommodation as a means of obtaining permanent resident status! Such schemes are rarely successful, and you could have problems in the future which could prevent you from ever living in the United States. Moreover, visa fraud is a federal crime for both you and the U.S. citizen spouse. A common INS tactic is to threaten the citizen with prosecution so he will testify against the alien spouse.

First Preference: Unmarried Sons and Daughters of U.S. Citizens

This category has 23,400 visas allocated annually and is usually current for countries other than Mexico and the Philippines, meaning that there is no backlog in issuance of visas. A petition on INS form I-130 must be filed at an INS Regional Service Center by the U.S. citizen parent.

If the category is current and the alien relative is legally in the United States, the visa petition can be filed at a local INS district office along with the alien relative's application for adjustment of status.

Second Preference A: Spouses and Minor Children of Permanent Residents

In a rather complicated quota allocation, this category has been allotted about 88,000 visas annually, 75% of which will be granted without reference to standard per-country limitations, benefiting natives of those countries with lengthy quota waits such as Mexico and the Philippines.

The permanent resident spouse or parent must file the visa petition with the INS on INS form I-130 as in First Preference applications.

The first through fourth preferences combined have over 226,000 visas allocated annually.

Second Preference B: Adult Unmarried Sons and Daughters of Permanent Residents

This category has been allotted at least 26,266 visas. The petition requirement is the same as Second Preference A.

Third Preference: Married Sons and Daughters of U.S. Citizens

This category has 23,400 visas allocated to it annually, which is less than demand, so a backlog should be expected. The petition requirement is the same as in the first and second preferences.

Fourth Preference: Brothers and Sisters of U.S. Citizens

Only adult citizens over the age of 21 may apply for relatives in this category. There are 65,000 visas available annually, and the backlog for this category is lengthy, probably in excess of fifteen years. The petition requirement is the same as for other family categories.

Employment-based Immigration

The aim of employment-based immigration is to encourage the immigration of highly trained and talented people.

There are five categories, called Preferences, of employment-based immigrant visas. The overall aim of this portion of the law is to encourage the immigration of highly trained and talented people or persons whose immigration will create employment for U.S. citizens.

Unless otherwise noted, the first three preferences require that a Petition for Prospective Immigrant Employee, INS form I-140, be filed with an INS regional service center before the alien can apply for the visa, and the second and third preferences further require that the prospective employer obtain an opinion, known as a Labor Certification, from the DOL that hiring the alien will not adversely affect U.S. workers.

Up to 40,000 visas are available annually for the first three, with up to 10,000 visas available for each of the fourth and fifth.

First Preference (Priority Workers)

1A: Extraordinary Ability

Aliens who can demonstrate extraordinary ability in the sciences, arts, education, business, or athletics are eligible to apply for an immigrant visa in this category. Such aliens must provide documentation of sustained national or international acclaim, such as receipt of a major international award or other evidence of achievement and renown. In addition, the entry of such a person must "substantially benefit" the U.S.

Aliens who can demonstrate extraordinary ability are eligible to apply for category 1A visa.

An alien claiming extraordinary ability must file a petition with an INS regional service center on INS form I-140; he may file on his own behalf without employer sponsorship, and no labor certification is required. A company can also file a petition for an employee who meets the requirements.

1B: Outstanding Professors and Researchers

Applicants for visas in this category must be coming to the United States to work for a university or to conduct research for a private company which is involved in full-time research activities and which has documented accomplishments in an academic field. The visa petition is filed with the INS by the university or the research company. A university professor must demonstrate three years teaching experience which was actual teaching and not just graduate assistantship-type experience.

1C: Multinational Executives and Managers

This category is the immigrant parallel to the L-1 non-immigrant category. A petition must be filed on INS form I-140 by the employer for the alien beneficiary to work in the U.S. in an executive or managerial capacity. The prospective employee must have been employed outside the U.S. (by the same employer or an affiliate or subsidiary) for at least one year within the immediately preceding three year period. The U.S. petitioner must have been engaged in active business operations for at least one year.

Second Preference

2A: Advanced Degrees

In order to qualify for this category, an alien must have a degree beyond a bachelor's degree, such as a master's degree or a Ph.D., and an approved INS I-140 petition by an employer for a job that requires the advanced degree.

The employee can demonstrate the equivalent of an advanced degree by having at least a bachelor's degree plus five years of progressive experience in the profession. No substitution of experience for a bachelor's degree will be allowed. A foreign bachelor's degree must be evaluated by an independent organization and found to be equivalent to a U.S. degree.

2B: Exceptional Ability

This category is for aliens of special ability,

but at a lesser level than "extraordinary." In order to show exceptional ability in the arts, sciences, or business, the alien must be able to demonstrate a degree of expertise significantly above the ordinary. These are document intensive petitions.

If it would be in the national interest to waive the requirement of a specific offer of employment, the alien may file his own petition on INS form I-140, and will not need a job offer or labor certification. It is unclear what will constitute national interest but some documentation of the positive nature of the alien's contribution to the U.S. economy or society will probably suffice.

To show exceptional ability, the alien must be able to demonstrate expertise significantly above the ordinary.

Third Preference

3A: Professionals

To qualify for this category, an alien must have at least a bachelor's degree and must have an employment offer which requires a degree. The INS requires that the alien actually have a degree; equivalent experience may not be substituted.

3B: Skilled Workers

Petitions for positions in this category must demonstrate that the job offered requires a minimum of two years of training or experience. The job cannot be temporary or seasonal.

3C: Other Workers

This category includes those permanent jobs such as manual labor or domestic work that require less than two years of training or experience and is limited to 10,000 visas annually. Visa petitions for these positions must be accompanied by a labor certification. There currently is a lengthy quota backlog. Many lawyers predict an eight year wait for visas in this category.

Fourth Preference: Religious Workers

There are 10,000 visas available annually in this category, covering three kinds of religious workers: 1) Ministers of religion; 2) professionals working in a religious vocation or occupation; and 3) other religious workers. The latter two sub-categories will be eliminated on October 1, 1994, and until then are limited to 5,000 of the total visas to be issued.

A visa petition on INS form I-360 must first be filed by the alien or any person on behalf of the alien with the INS. All applicants must have held membership in a U.S. nonprofit religious denomination and must have worked in the vocation for at least two years immediately preceding the filing of the petition. In addition, the alien must demonstrate that he is coming to the U.S. solely for the purpose of serving as a minister of that religious denomination or to work in a professional or other capacity for the denomination or its affiliated non-profit organization.

The employment creation visa makes it possible for 10,000 people annually to obtain LPR status.

Fifth Preference: Investors

This visa category, also called the "employment creation" visa, makes it possible for 10,000 persons annually to obtain LPR status if they can meet the investment and employment creation level the law requires.

In order to qualify, an applicant must make a capital investment of one million dollars (or at least $500,000, if investing in a low-employment target area identified by the DOL) in a new (begun after November 26, 1990) business enterprise in the U.S. which will provide full-time employment for at least ten persons who are unrelated to the immigrant investor.

If the petition, filed on INS form I-526 is approved, the investor will be granted conditional status, which will be upgraded to permanent after two years, upon a showing that the investment has actually met the requirements of the law. There are currently no regulations or forms regarding the process to remove the conditional aspect of the status.

Asylees and Refugees

This method of obtaining entry into the United States is available only under circumstances dictated by Congress and is applicable only to persons fleeing persecution in their native land. The following discussion is abbreviated, but there are many organizations in the United States which assist refugees and applicants for asylum, and you should contact such an organization in your area. The local INS office should have a list of non-profit organizations which can assist you.

There are many organizations in the United States which assist refugees and applicants for asylum.

Refugees

Refugee status is only available to persons who are outside the United States. The number of refugees to be admitted each year is determined by a consultative process between various government agencies, based on current political and humanitarian priorities.

A refugee is someone who is unable or unwilling to return to his country of nationality due to persecution or a well-founded fear of persecution on account of his race, religion, nationality, membership in a particular social group, or political opinion. Persons who have participated in the persecution of others may not obtain refugee status.

Refugees must be admissible under the exclusion provisions of the law, and are usually pre-screened by the State Department or some assistance organization. The number allowed to enter each year is governed by Congress and the President. Historically, the large majority of refugee admissions have been from Communist countries such as Hungary, the Soviet Union and Viet Nam, but this is changing and now many refugees are from Africa.

Applications for admission as a refugee are managed by the State Department of the United States, often in conjunction with the United Nations High Commissioner for Refugees. The procedures vary widely and are outside the scope of this book. Persons admitted as refugees must wait one year after entry before they are allowed to apply for permanent resident status.

Asylees

Asylum status is available only to persons who are inside the United States or who are applying for admission at a border. The application may be made affirmatively with the INS, or as a request for relief from deportation during proceedings in front of an immigration judge, when it is usually combined with a request for withholding of deportation, a technical ground of relief from deportation which is similar to asylum. The applicant must meet the definition of refugee described above, and must convince the INS or the judge that he is deserving of the status, since the granting of an application for asylum is discretionary on the part of the U.S. government. Persons convicted of aggravated felonies, and persons who have assisted in the persecution of others may not be granted asylum.

The application is made on INS form I-589 and should be filed with as much supporting documentation as possible, including a lengthy affidavit detailing the applicant's history.

The granting of an application for asylum is discretionary on the part of the U.S. government.

If an application for asylum is granted, the alien must wait at least one year before making application for LPR status with the INS. Immediate family members may join the successful asylum applicant in the United States.

Miscellaneous Categories

Humanitarian and political considerations have been the impetus for a number of unusual provisions allowing immigrant entries.

Displaced Tibetans

Between October 1, 1991 and September 30, 1994, 1,000 immigrant visas will be made available for native Tibetans and their children and grandchildren who are residing in India or Nepal. The visas are to be distributed in an equitable manner to those who are likely to be successfully resettled in the United States.

Diversity and Transitional Programs

These programs are authorized by Congress in an attempt to correct the consequences of the world-wide quota system and to allow additional immigration from certain under-represented countries. The rules can only be described as confusing, but they offer some relief from the numerical restrictions of the normal visa channels. The diversity visas (available beginning October 1, 1995) and diversity transition visas (October 1, 1992 through September 30, 1995) are often referred to as the "lottery" visas. Lottery visas are available only to natives of certain specified countries in annual amounts allocated by a formula that is almost incomprehensible. The actual awarding of these visas is administered according to procedures determined by the State Department.

Lottery visas are available only to natives of certain specified countries.

The application procedure will be publicized by the State Department each year, and interested persons should check with the State Department's Public Information Office in Washington D.C. for more information. The address and phone number are shown in Appendix A.

Hong Kong Provisions

The number of immigrant visas available to natives of Hong Kong was increased in 1990, and an independent category of quota numbers was established for certain employees of U.S. businesses.

In order to qualify as an employee of a U.S. business, the applicant must have been employed for one year in Hong Kong as an officer, supervisor, manager, executive, or in a capacity involving specialized knowledge, by a U.S. business entity or its subsidiary or affiliate. The business entity must employ at least 100 people in the United States and 50 people outside the United States, and must have a gross annual income of at least $50 million. Finally, the company must offer the alien employment in the U.S. in one of the capacities listed above.

Schedule A

Although most employment related visas require that the employer first demonstrate that there is no U.S. worker willing and available for the job, the DOL will waive the labor certification process for jobs it has pre-certified to have a shortage of workers. This is a valuable waiver because the labor certification process is so difficult.

The labor certification process is waived for certain jobs precertified to have a shortage of workers.

Jobs which qualify for Schedule A pre-certification still require visa petitions, but the burden of obtaining a labor certification has been lifted.

Group I of Schedule A pre-certifies two groups of health care professionals, registered nurses and physical therapists. Group II pre-certifies jobs for aliens of exceptional ability in the sciences or arts (excluding the performing arts), including college and university teachers.

The standard employment visa petition (INS form I-140) must be filed, accompanied by the DOL forms ETA 750A and ETA 750B.

Registry

Registry is a visa category which reveals the rarely seen heart of Congress in dealing with aliens. Registry is a kind of amnesty which legalizes the status of undocumented aliens who have lived in the United States for a long period of time. In order to register for permanent resident status, you must have entered the United States, either legally or illegally, before January 1, 1972 and must have maintained your U.S. residence continuously since that time. You apply by filing INS form I-485 at your local INS District Office. You must prove to the INS that you entered the United States before January of 1972. You may do this by showing an entry stamp in your passport, or you can bring dated documents such as school or medical records or rent receipts which show that you were here. You must also prove that your residence in the United States has been continuous, and that you did not leave the country for so long that you appear to have established a new residence elsewhere. Once again, dated documents showing that you have been living in the U.S. each year since 1972, along with affidavits from persons who have known you were here must be shown to the INS.

Registry is a visa category which reveals the rarely-seen heart of Congress.

If you have taken brief visits outside the country which you did not intend as abandonment of your home in the United States, your continuity of residence is not interrupted. However, you will have to convince the INS that each visit was brief and for a temporary purpose, such as to visit a relative or take a vacation or business trip. Any documents that you can find to support your claim of unabandoned residence will be of assistance.

Applicants for registry must show that they are of good moral character at the time of application. A showing of "good moral character" requires that you do more than bring letters of reference saying that you are a good person. It is defined in the law. You will not be eligible for registry if you have been convicted of certain crimes, if you have been in prison for a total period of more than 180 days, if you are a practicing polygamist, a habitual drunkard, a smuggler, if your income is derived principally from gambling, or if you have given false testimony to get an immigration benefit. Determination of whether you meet the statutory definition of good moral character can be complex. If you have any doubt, you must seek the advice of an experienced immigration attorney.

Applicants for registry must show that they are of good moral character.

Widows/Widowers

Widows and widowers of U.S. citizens who have been married for at least two years before the spouse died may file for permanent resident status after the death of the spouse. This benefit has been available only since November 29, 1990, but there is a transitional period making this application available to persons whose citizen spouse died before that date. The widow or widower of a U.S. citizen may apply for permanent residence even if the spouse died many years ago, if the application is made before November 29, 1992.

Application may be made on INS form 360 at the local INS District Office if the applicant is eligible for adjustment of status; otherwise it is filed with the appropriate Regional Service Center.

The widow or widower may not have remarried and must have been married to the U.S. citizen at the time of his death.

CHAPTER THREE
SEEKING ADMISSION:
CAN YOU COME IN?
....

Entry

The first requirement for entering the United States is having one of the visas described in Chapter Two. Persons who Congress has decided should not be allowed to enter the United States are classified as "excludible," and the immigration law contains a lengthy list of grounds of "excludibility."

> *Persons who Congress has decided should not be allowed to enter the United States are classified as "excludible."*

When applying for the visa at a U.S. Consulate, and again when asking the INS for entry at the border, you must demonstrate that you are not a member of one of the groups whose members the U.S. Congress has decided will not be allowed to enter the country. There are numerous grounds on which a person can be denied entry, although some can be waived if the applicant has close relatives who are legal residents or citizens.

In general, an alien may not enter the United States if he:

- has a communicable disease of public health significance (the Department of Health and Human Services publishes the list. Removal of HIV from the list is under consideration by the Clinton administration);

- has a physical or mental disorder that is a threat to others;

- is a drug abuser or drug addict;

- has been convicted of or admits to having committed a crime of moral turpitude (theft, fraud, child abuse, deliberate crimes of violence, to name only a few), unless there is only one such conviction or admission, and the alien was sentenced to only six months or less in jail;

- has been convicted of or admits to committing acts which constitute the essential elements of a violation of law relating to "controlled substances" (narcotics and drugs);

- has been convicted of two or more crimes for which the aggregate prison sentences were more than five years;

- is "reasonably believed" by the INS to be a drug trafficker (no conviction is necessary);

- is coming to the U.S. to engage in prostitution directly or indirectly, or has been engaged in prostitution within ten years of application for a visa;

- is entering to engage in espionage, sabotage or terrorist activities;

- has been a member of a communist or totalitarian party (although there are exceptions for involuntary or past membership and for close family members of U.S. residents);

- was a participant in Nazi persecutions;

- is likely to become a public charge;

An alien may not enter the United States if he is reasonably believed by the INS to be a drug trafficker.

- is coming to practice medicine and is a graduate of a foreign medical school (does not apply to Canadians);

- has been excluded and deported within the past year, has been deported within the past five years, or is accompanying such a person;

- has tried to obtain or has obtained a visa or entry into the U.S. by deliberately misrepresenting or lying about an important fact (this includes persons who have attempted to obtain an immigrant visa by entering into a sham marriage);

- is a stowaway;

- has been convicted of using false immigration documents;

- has been a draft evader in the U.S.;

- is a practicing polygamist; or

- has violated a child custody order by taking or keeping a child outside the U.S.

If you fit into one of these categories, you will not be allowed to enter the U.S.

If you fit into one of these categories, you will not be allowed to enter the U.S. either by the State Department, which will not issue a visa, or by the INS, which will not let you enter the country. However, you may qualify for a waiver of the rule which would otherwise prohibit your entry. An application for a waiver is filed on INS form I-601.

For example, the communicable disease ground can be waived if you are the spouse, son or daughter of a citizen or lawful permanent resident, or if you are already a lawful permanent resident and you have a spouse, son, or daughter who is a citizen or lawful permanent resident.

If you are likely to be denied entry because of a criminal conviction, one of the relationships described above could constitute grounds for a waiver, unless the conviction involved drugs, murder or torture. If your conviction occured more than 15 years ago, or if it was for possession of less than 30 grams of marijuana, you may be granted a waiver if you can show that a) you have been rehabilitated, and b) denial of your entry to the U.S. would result in hardship to your U.S. citizen relative(s).

Finally, if you are excludible because of fraud committed regarding the entry or immigration processes, you may apply for a waiver if you can show that you have one of the relationships described above, that the fraud occurred more than ten years ago, and if you can demonstrate that your entry will not be contrary to the national welfare or safety.

It is important to read the visa application carefully. Answer each question truthfully and accurately. One false answer could affect your ability to travel to or live in the U.S. forever. You may wish to seek expert advice if you believe you fall into one of the categories which mandates denial of entry.

It is important to read the visa application carefully. Answer each question truthfully and accurately.

Where Do You Apply to Enter?

There are three instances when an official will determine whether you may enter the U.S. The first will occur when you go to a U.S. consulate to apply for a visa; the second when you actually attempt to enter the U.S at a port of entry; the third time when an INS official rules on an application for adjustment of status.

The U.S. Consulate

Non-immigrant Visa Applications

The State Department's application for admission as a non-immigrant is the form OF-156. It asks you to answer a number of questions about the grounds of exclusion. If you answer yes to any of the questions, the consular officer will need to question you further to determine whether you may be admitted to the U.S. and, if you are not eligible to enter, whether a waiver is available. If the consular officer tells you that you may not be admitted and declines to give you a visa, there is very little you can do. Be sure that you understand why you have been denied a visa, and ask the consular officer for a written decision that tells you why the visa was denied.

It will do no good to try again at a different Consulate. The officer at the first Consulate will have noted the refusal and reason for it in the State Department's computer database, and that information will be available to other Consulates. In addition, one of the questions on the OF-156 asks that you explain any past visa refusals, and it is always extremely important to answer each question truthfully and accurately.

You may, however, reapply for the visa and attempt to overcome the reason for the denial. For example, if the consular officer has denied a request for a B-2 tourist visa because he believes that you will not return to your home country, you may be able to convince him that

Be sure that you understand why you have been denied a visa, and ask the consular officer for a written decision that tells you why the visa was denied.

you have sufficient ties to your home to demonstrate that you will return. You may want to bring documents showing your financial ties, such as deeds to land, proof of business ownership, etc., or you may explain that because your family is not traveling with you, you will have to return. The consular officer's main concern is usually whether or not you will abide by the terms of your visa and return in a timely manner to your home country.

If the consular officer continues to refuse to grant the visa, you have no recourse. United States Consulates have nearly unassailable authority with respect to the issuance of visas. Some Consulates, for example, will not even accept a new application for six months after a denial. As a non-citizen outside the borders of the U.S. you do not have the protection of the U.S. Constitution or the courts, and you have no right to enter the United States.

If the consular officer continues to refuse to grant the visa, you have no recourse.

Immigrant Visa Application

The process for obtaining an immigrant visa is much more complex. Once the Consulate has received notice that an immigrant visa petition filed by your relative or employer has been approved, you will be sent a packet of forms and instructions. The process may take as long as 90 days, because you must provide the Consulate with police certificates from each place you have lived for six months or more since you reached the age of sixteen, in order to demonstrate that you may not be denied entry under any of the criminal grounds. You must also provide the Consulate with proof that you will not become a public charge, and submit to a medical exam to demonstrate that you are not inadmissible under any of the medical grounds. Eventually, you will be given an interview date. That is when the decision will be made granting or denying the permanent resident visa.

Port of Entry

Once the visa stamp is placed in your passport and you are at the border, whether in an airport or at a land border, you will be asking an official of the Immigration and Naturalization Service, usually an immigration "inspector," to admit you to the United States. You must show the inspector the visa stamp in your passport or alien registration receipt card, unless you are applying for entry under a visa waiver program. You may be questioned about your intended activities in the U.S. if you are applying for entry as a non-immigrant. If you have an immigrant visa or an Alien Registration Card, you may be questioned to determine if you are a returning resident with an unabandoned residence in the U.S.

If you are denied admission at a port of entry, you have the option of asking for a hearing.

If you are denied admission at a port of entry, you have the option of asking for a hearing in front of an immigration judge, during which you can renew your request for entry. At the hearing, you can be represented by an attorney, at your own expense. You have the right to a fair hearing but you do not have the full constitutional protection of someone who is inside the U.S. because you are only an applicant for entry. Even though you are physically within the borders of the U.S., for purposes of the hearing you are considered to be "outside." Further, if the judge decides that you may not be admitted, the law requires that you be "deported," and you may not re-enter the country for one year. This provision can be waived, and the INS can agree to let you re-enter prior to the end of the one year if you have close family in the U.S.

Adjustment of Status

"Adjustment" of status is a procedure by which a non-immigrant alien may apply to have his non-immigrant status changed to immigrant status. It is not the same as "change" of status, which is the process used to change from one non-immigrant status to another non-immigrant status. "Adjustment" is an entry procedure which applies to immigrant visa applicants only. Normally all visas, including immigrant visas, must be applied for and obtained from the State Department at a U.S. Consulate outside the U.S. The adjustment process, however, allows you to get your permanent resident visa without leaving the United States. Not only is this often more convenient, but if the INS denies the application, there is an appeal process available. There is no appeal of a consular officer's decision to deny a visa.

The adjustment process allows you to get your permanent resident visa without leaving the U.S.

This important benefit is not available to all aliens who can otherwise qualify for permanent resident status. You must have legally entered the United States, must not have engaged in unauthorized employment at any time, must not have overstayed your allotted time, must be admissible, and an immigrant visa must be immediately available (i.e., you must be an immediate relative, or you must have a "current" priority date).

Making a determination of your eligibility for adjustment can be difficult, and you may need the advice of an attorney. The rules are complicated. Certain classes of aliens, including crew members and aliens allowed to enter the country only because they are in transit to another country, are not allowed to apply, and certain others apply under special rules. In addition, some of the grounds of excludibility are automatically waived for certain national groups admitted to the U.S. under special procedures.

The process is similar to the immigrant visa application process at a U.S. Consulate abroad. The paperwork differs slightly and will be on INS forms, but the goal is to prove to the INS that you are not within any of the grounds which would forbid your entry if you were outside the United States, and that you should be allowed to enter the United States as an immigrant.

Visa Status

The activities in which you are allowed to engage are determined by your visa status.

The activities in which you are allowed to engage in the U.S. are determined by your visa status. If you get a visa and are allowed to enter in one of the non-immigrant categories, a white card will be stapled in your passport by the inspector. This is the INS form I-94. It is your record of admission and tells you what status you have in the United States. Usually you will have the status authorized by the visa stamp. The I-94 form also will tell you how long you may remain in the U.S. It is not a visa, and it may show that your status will end long before your visa stamp expires. While you are inside the United States, the I-94 form governs your status. You must either leave or apply for an extension before it expires. If you remain in the U.S.

past the expiration date of the I-94, you will be "out of status" and subject to deportation.

Once you are in the United States, you are subject to the rules of the visa category in which you entered. If you engage in activities that are inconsistent with your entry status, you will be out of status and subject to deportation. For example, if your I-94 status is that of a student at a university, you may not accept off-campus employment without the express permission of the INS, nor may you attend another university without first having obtained the INS' permission to transfer. Because your legal presence in the U.S. is always dependent upon your compliance with the terms of your visa status, you should be sure that you understand the requirements of your visa. For example, some consular officers believe that a B visa was fraudulently obtained if the alien accepted unauthorized employment in the U.S. within thirty days of entry.

U.S. Laws

You will be subject to U.S. laws, including those that govern the payment of income taxes.

There are certain legal requirements that non-immigrants share with all citizens and permanent residents of the United States. You will be subject to U.S. laws and regulations, including those that govern the payment of personal income taxes and the filing of tax returns. This book does not cover the technicalities of income tax requirements, but the general rule is that if you are physically present inside the U.S. for certain periods of time you will be considered to be a "tax resident" and will be subject to the tax laws of this country. Whether or not you are a tax resident is absolutely unrelated to your immigration status, unless you are here on a student visa or you are an LPR. Failure to pay taxes will not affect your immigration status, but will cause other problems, and you should not ignore the laws in that area.

Employment Authorization

Before being hired, workers in the United States must prove that they are authorized to work. All citizens and permanent residents are authorized to work without any restrictions. However, this is not true for non-immigrant aliens. While in the U.S. in any non-immigrant status, your right to work is dependent upon the terms of your visa status. Some visa categories do not allow employment of any kind. It is against the law for employers to hire persons who are not permitted to work, and all new employees in the U.S. must fill out a form and give evidence of work authorization at the time of hire.

Your right to work is dependent upon the terms of your visa status.

Your ability to accept employment is governed by the terms of your visa status, which will also affect your ability to obtain a social security card. The Social Security Administration will endorse cards issued to persons whose visas do not allow unrestricted employment with the notation "Not to be Used for Employment." Evidence of U.S. citizenship, permanent residence, or an INS-issued work authorization card, the EAD (Employment Authorization Document), must be shown in order to obtain an unmarked card. The social security number itself is unaffected by any notation and will be your permanent number.

Obtaining an EAD is possible only in limited and restricted circumstances. If you do not have a visa that specifically allows you to accept employment in the U.S. and you wish to work, you must first obtain the appropriate visa, if possible. If you are employed in the U.S. without permission to work you will be out of status and subject to deportation. Only in very limited circumstances may persons obtain work authorization by making application at the INS office nearest their residence. These circumstances are described on the back of the INS form I-765, along with the eligibility requirement, which may include demonstration of financial need.

Once you are inside the U.S., you will be subject to the terms of your non immigrant visa category.

SUMMARY

Admission to the United States requires that both the Department of State and the INS agree that you are eligible to enter. Once you have been admitted and are inside the U.S., you will be subject to the strict terms of your non-immigrant visa category and the time limitation of your authorized stay. If you do not remain in legal status, you are subject to deportation.

CHAPTER FOUR
THE "GREEN CARD": WHAT DOES IT MEAN?

Lawful Permanent Residence

A lawful permanent resident is an individual who has been legally admitted to the United States as an immigrant. Other names for immigrated aliens include "resident alien," "LPR," "green card holder," and "permanent resident." Permanent residents are not citizens; they are "aliens," but they have the privilege of residing permanently in the United States, are able to work without restriction, and are protected by the United States Constitution and the laws of the states and the federal government.

When permanent resident status is granted by a U.S. consulate, a stamp evidencing the status is placed in your passport. The stamp is good for four months, and you must enter the United States before it expires. If you became a permanent resident pursuant to an application for adjustment of status in the U.S., as described in Chapter Three, you will symbolically "enter" the U.S. at the time of the interview at the INS office. The INS may give you a written notice that the application for permanent resident status has been granted, but this can be used only as a work authorization document. It cannot be used as a re-entry document after travel abroad. The INS will, however, place a stamp in your passport which serves as temporary evidence of your new status, and which will allow you to re-enter the U.S. after travel abroad.

A lawful permanent resident is an individual who has been legally admitted to the United States as an immigrant.

After three or four months you will receive your Alien Registration Card in the mail. It is your permanent evidence of status, and will have your picture, a fingerprint, and alien registration number on it. The alien registration number, also called the "A" number, is an eight digit number preceded by an "A" and will be your identification number for any future dealings with the INS. The card will have an expiration date ten years from the date of entry, requiring that the card be reissued. Although the card expires, your permanent resident status does not expire.

Persons who obtained immigrant status as immigrant investors or based on a marriage to a U.S. citizen of less than two years duration will receive a different card, showing that their status is "conditional." It will have an expiration date two years from the date of entry. See the discussion in Chapter Two.

Resident aliens enjoy the protections of the U.S. Constitution.

Resident aliens enjoy the protection of the U.S. Constitution regarding such important rights as free speech, free press, due process of law, religious expression and practice, and freedom from unlawful search and seizure. In addition, they may petition for immigrant status for their spouses and children, and may provide those relatives with eligibility for waivers of excludibility, if needed, as described in Chapter Two. Eventually resident aliens may apply to become naturalized citizens of the U.S., if the preliminary requirements are met, as described in Chapter Six. However aliens may not vote, may not serve on juries, and remain subject to deportation.

It is unlawful for employers to discriminate in the hiring process against any prospective employee because of national origin or citizenship status. However, LPRs may expect to find legal restrictions on the employment of non-citizens in certain government positions, and the U.S. Constitution forbids the election of aliens as President, Vice-President, Senator, or Representative.

Permanent resident aliens are tax residents of the U.S. and must file U.S. income tax returns on their world-wide income. This responsibility does not cease unless permanent resident status is lost.

Loss of Permanent Resident Status

Permanent resident status is not necessarily permanent.

There are a number of ways in which a permanent resident alien can lose his status, but only the most important involuntary ways to lose status are discussed in this chapter. Once lost, LPR status can be regained only by beginning the immigrant visa application process again. It is extremely important to understand that permanent resident status is not necessarily "permanent."

Abandonment

After you become a permanent resident, you must demonstrate at the time of any re-entry that your trip outside the United States was "temporary," and that you are returning to your unabandoned primary residence. If you remain outside the United States for a lengthy period or engage in activities which indicate that your permanent residence is no longer inside the U.S., the INS may consider you to have voluntarily given up your status as a permanent resident of the U.S., and attempt to deny your entry.

It is a common fallacy that brief annual trips to the United States will prevent loss of LPR status. This is absolutely untrue. If your actual permanent residence is not in the United States, you have abandoned your immigrant status.

It is a common fallacy that brief annual trips to the United States will prevent loss of LPR status.

The factors determining the "temporariness" of any trips outside the U.S. include the following:

- Is your actual home and place of employment in the United States?

- Did you have a definite temporary reason to travel abroad?

- Did you expect to return within a relatively short period of time?

- Are you returning when expected? If not, what circumstances caused you to spend additional time abroad? Were they within your control?

- Where are your family ties, property, business affiliations, etc.?

- Have you filed U.S. resident tax returns?

If the INS inspector at the port of entry is not satisfied that you qualify as a returning permanent resident, you may be "paroled" into the country, that is allowed to enter physically although legally considered to be "outside" in order to allow the local INS office to conduct a "deferred" inspection. This means that the INS has deferred or postponed consideration of your application for entry until a later date. You will be asked to appear at an INS office inside the country. A deferred inspection actually consists of an interview. During the interview, you will be allowed to present evidence which has a bearing on whether your U.S. residence has been abandoned.

Alternatively, the INS may deny entry and classify you as one who no longer has a status which allows entry into the United States.

Because permanent residence is such a valuable right, it may not be taken away by the INS without the due process guaranteed by the U.S. Constitution. As a returning resident, you may renew your application for entry at an "exclusion" hearing in front of an immigration judge by asking for a hearing in which to present evidence demonstrating that you have not abandoned your U.S. residence. You may be represented by a lawyer, at your own expense.

Permanent residence may not be taken away by the INS without the due process guaranteed by the U.S. Constitution.

You may withdraw your application for entry at any time and return to your point of departure outside the United States. In fact, INS officials promote this solution, which unfortunately has serious repercussions if you wish to be considered to be a returning resident. Withdrawal of your application to enter as a permanent resident will be viewed by the INS as an admission of abandonment, and you will no longer be a permanent resident. Do not be intimidated! Insist on a hearing, and time to consult a lawyer.

A request for a hearing also may have unintended consequences, as you may be held in custody unless the INS agrees to your release pending commencement of the hearing. Persons in exclusion proceedings do not have a right to be released, and it is within the discretion of the immigration judge and the INS whether to release you, and if so, to require that a bond be posted.

During the hearing, you may present evidence that your trip abroad was temporary and that your U.S. residence has not been abandoned. Once you have demonstrated some evidence that you are a returning resident, usually by showing your Alien Registration Card, the burden of proof is on the INS to demonstrate that you should not be admitted. The INS will attempt to show that your actions demonstrated an intent to live permanently outside the United States or that you fall within one of the classes of people who are forbidden to enter. You must prove otherwise.

An unfavorable decision by the immigration judge may be appealed to the Board of Immigration Appeals, and thereafter to a federal district court.

If the final result is a determination that you are not a returning resident, you will be excluded and deported from the United States, and may not re-enter for one year.

Deportation and Exclusion

As with non-immigrants, permanent resident aliens are in the United States pursuant to the law governing their status. Laws are always subject to change and LPRs must remember that the conditions of their stay are not immutable, and further that violation of the governing statutes will place their status at risk.

Permenent residents must remember that violation of the governing statutes will place their status at risk.

Congress has described certain behavior that will subject aliens to deportation, as well as behavior which will subject aliens to exclusion if engaged in prior to an attempt to enter the U.S. These are separate sections of the immigration law. Exclusion is discussed in Chapter Three; deportation is discussed in Chapter Five.

Congress has described certain behavior that will subject aliens to deportation.

For example, a permanent resident alien who is convicted of a crime that is included in the law's list of deportable offenses may be involuntarily removed, or deported, from the U.S. after a deportation hearing. A final determination by an immigration judge that you must be deported terminates your permanent resident status, and you will be sent back to your native country.

Similarly, an attempt to enter after actions that constitute a ground of excludibility may result in a final order of exclusion, which will prevent your return to the United States and also terminate your resident status. For example, suppose a permanent resident travels abroad to traffic in cocaine. If the INS has reasonably believable knowledge of this behavior, the alien will be refused entry into the United States, and will lose his permanent resident status.

Thus, permanent resident aliens retain their status subject to their obedience to the statutory requirements of that status. This is not true for citizens, including naturalized citizens, who have a nearly absolute right to reside in the United States and to re-enter after any absence.

Rescission

Resident aliens who entered the U.S. through

adjustment of status may lose their resident status if, within five years of the date of the adjustment interview, the INS can demonstrate in a hearing before an immigration judge that the alien was not in fact entitled to receive permanent resident status at the time. Such hearings are called "rescission" hearings because the INS is trying to "rescind" or undo its original grant of status.

For example, an alien who obtained permanent resident status based on a fraudulent marriage may find the INS attempting to undo the award of permanent residence by showing the immigration judge evidence to demonstrate that the marriage was a sham. If the INS is successful, the alien will be subject to deportation because he will no longer have a visa. Although there is a five year limitation on the INS' right to attempt to undo a grant of permanent status, the reason for rescission will usually also be a separate ground of deportability, so the INS may institute deportation proceedings if the discovery of fraud is made after the five year period.

The "green card" offers limited rights with respect to residency in the United States.

SUMMARY

The "green card" offers limited rights with respect to residency in the United States, and resident aliens are subject to loss of their ability to live and work in the United States if they do not pay careful attention to the terms and conditions of their permanent resident status. Keeping your permanent resident status is also important because it is the first step to obtaining U.S. citizenship.

CHAPTER FIVE
DEPORTATION:
CAN YOU BE SENT HOME?

Who Can Be Deported?

Only "aliens" who have actually entered the United States can be deported or sent back to their country of origin. Citizens cannot be deported and aliens outside the United States can only be prevented from entering. Some of the activities that can cause the INS to begin deportation proceedings against you may seem inconsequential, but the deportation laws can be harsh and must be treated with respect.

Except where the President or Congress has made specific provision otherwise, the rules governing when a person can be deported are applicable to all aliens, whether living in the United States legally or illegally, and whether they are here on non-immigrant visas or as lawful permanent residents.

From time to time, the President exempts certain classes of aliens from deportation.

There are a few temporary exceptions to the deportation rules. From time to time, the President exempts certain classes of aliens from deportation, usually for humanitarian reasons. Currently, there are restrictions on the forced removal of citizens of El Salvador, Liberia, Lebanon, Afghanistan, Poland, China, and Somalia, including stateless aliens who last habitually resided in any of the designated countries. These provisions are temporary and subject to change. If you have questions about whether any of these temporary humanitarian rules may apply to you, contact the U.S. State Department or an experienced immigration attorney.

Grounds of Deportation

The United States does not permit aliens who engage in criminal activities or who violate the immigration law to remain in the country. The grounds of deportation listed below demonstrate the intent of the Congress to expel aliens whose behavior is undesirable:

- Any alien who could have been prevented from entering at the time of his last entry is deportable, as is any alien who entered at a place other than a regulated port of entry, often referred to as "entering without inspection," or EWI. Entering through a hole in the fence or in any way that avoids presenting yourself to a border official, or that involves fraud or misrepresentation is absolutely foolish.

- Any alien who violates the terms of his visa status can be deported.

- Aliens who obtained their visas by fraud can be deported. This includes those who obtained LPR status by marrying a U.S. citizen, whose marriage was annulled or terminated within two years, and who can not establish that the marriage was not entered into for the purpose of evading the immigration laws.

- An alien who is a "conditional" resident based upon marriage to a U.S. citizen or who obtained such status as an immigrant investor, and whose conditional sta-

Any alien who violates the terms of his visa status can be deported.

61

tus has been terminated by the INS can be deported.

- Any alien who knowingly engaged in the smuggling of other aliens into the U.S. can be deported, whether or not the activity was undertaken for gain. (There is a waiver available if the persons smuggled were immediate relatives of the alien.)

- An alien convicted of a crime involving "moral turpitude," which includes fraud, theft, and other morally reprehensible crimes, if the crime was committed within five years after entry and the alien is either sentenced to or serves one year in confinement, can be deported.

- Also deportable are those aliens who are convicted of two or more crimes of moral turpitude at any time after entry.

- An alien convicted of an aggravated felony can be deported. Aggravated felonies are: murder, drug trafficking, illegal dealing in firearms or destructive devices and, if committed after November 29, 1990, money laundering, and crimes of violence for which a five year sentence was imposed. Foreign convictions for those offenses will be considered to be "aggravated" if a term of imprisonment was completed within the last fifteen years.

- An alien convicted of any drug offense can be deported, unless he has only one conviction for simple possession of 30 grams or less of marijuana.

- Aliens who are, or who at any time after

entry have been drug abusers or drug addicts can be deported.

- Any alien convicted at any time after entry of a violation of a firearm law can be deported.

- Failure to properly register change of address with the INS may make an alien deportable, unless the failure was reasonably excusable or was not willful. The INS is preparing a new form for registration of address change.

- Aliens convicted of violations of federal laws relating to fraud and misuse of visas, permits, and other entry documents can be deported.

- Aliens convicted of violations of certain federal statutes, including the Foreign Agents Registration Act, the Trading With the Enemy Act, and the Military Selective Service Act, can also be deported.

- Any alien who has become a public charge within five years of entry for reasons which existed at the time of entry can be deported.

- Aliens who pose a security risk, including spies, saboteurs and terrorists, can be deported.

- Aliens who have been involved in Nazi persecutions (between March 23, 1933 and May 8, 1945), or who have engaged in conduct defined as genocide can be deported.

- Finally, an alien whose presence or activity in the U.S. is reasonably believed by the Secretary of State to have "potentially serious" foreign policy consequences can be deported.

From time to time, Congress changes the reasons why persons can be deported, so this list may not be current. In addition, the issues surrounding an INS claim that a person should be deported will have many complexities which a book of this length cannot address. If you have a question regarding whether or not you can be deported, seek competent advice. This is a highly technical and complicated area of the law, and a misunderstanding or an error could affect your right to remain in or to re-enter the United States.

From time to time, Congress changes the reasons why persons can be deported.

Relief From Deportation

Because deportation is such a harsh penalty, the law provides some relief from its effects. In addition, some of the deportation rules can be waived if the requirements for waiver are met. Waivers were discussed in the descriptions of specific grounds of deportability. Most of the avenues of relief, however, are limited to very specific circumstances and depend upon the discretion of an immigration judge.

Expungement/Pardon

If the reason for deportation is conviction of a crime, removal of the conviction will often remove that ground of deportability.

If a conviction of a crime involving moral turpitude is "expunged" under state law procedures (foreign expungements are not effective), the conviction can not be used to deport you. Expungement is a method of removing the crime from your record. If it is available for a particular crime, it is essential that the state expungement law remove the crime from your record as though you had not been convicted. Expungement may not be available for certain types of crimes. The expungement rules which will apply will be those of the state in which the conviction occurred. If expungement is possible, the immigration judge should postpone deportation proceedings to allow you to apply for the order of expungement.

However, even if the law allows expungement of a narcotics conviction, you can still be deported. Drug convictions are considered to be so serious that there is no relief from deportation. The only exception is a federal statute, the Comprehensive Crime Control Act, which has an expungement provision for certain youthful first offenders. This is a very limited exception. State expungement statutes which are similar to the Comprehensive Crime Control Act may also provide relief from a simple drug possession conviction and keep you from being deported, but whether or not a state's statute qualifies is a question for an expert in immigration law.

Drug convictions are considered to be so serious that there is no relief from deportation.

A full and unconditional pardon by the President, or the governor of a state can also keep you from being deported, but only from criminal convictions that do not include drugs. Foreign pardons are not effective to bar deportation due to drug crimes.

There are a number of miscellaneous methods to eliminate a conviction which are beyond the scope of this book. They include the rarely used legal writs of audita querela and error coram nobis, motions to withdraw a plea, or to correct or reduce a sentence, and a writ of habeas corpus to vacate or set aside a conviction. Obviously the advice and assistance of an attorney will be needed to assist with these more unusual solutions.

Voluntary Departure

Voluntary departure, also known as "voluntary return," is the most common relief from being deported; it does not allow you to remain in the United States. Voluntary departure is your agreement with the INS that you will leave voluntarily and at your own expense, and the INS will not have you deported, even though you have violated the law regarding your stay or your entry into the United States.

Voluntary departure is your agreement with the INS that you will leave voluntarily and at your own expense.

There is no application form; you may make the request directly to the INS or to the judge during your deportation hearing.

There are three statutory requirements for a grant of voluntary departure: "good moral character" for the preceding five years, willingness to leave the United States voluntarily, and ability to pay the expense of the trip home.

"Good moral character" is defined in the statute. Persons who have committed a crime of moral turpitude, multiple crimes, or drug crimes (unless it is only one conviction for simple possession of 30 grams or less of marijuana), or who have been imprisoned as a result of any conviction for an aggregate period of 180 days or more, or who have been convicted of an aggravated felony during the five year period, are barred from establishing good moral character, and are ineligible for voluntary departure. Also ineligible are practicing polygamists, habitual drunkards, smugglers, persons whose income is derived principally from gambling or who have been convicted of two or more gambling offenses, and persons who have given false testimony to obtain an immigration benefit.

However, even if the statutory bars to good moral character as listed above do not apply, the judge may still deny a request for voluntary departure, based upon his discretion. You can be deported based upon the judge's belief that you do not have good moral character. An alien's general conduct with respect to the laws of the United States may be taken into account by the judge. For example, a history of illegal entries may influence the judge's exercise of discretion.

An alien's general conduct with respect to the laws of the United States may be taken into account by the judge.

Voluntary departure is a benefit and you must abide by its terms. Failure to leave on or before your voluntary departure date can disqualify you from eligibility for several of the kinds of relief from being deported discussed in this chapter, including voluntary return, for a period of five years.

Suspension of Deportation

Suspension of deportation is available to aliens who have resided in the United States continuously for a long period of time, and who will suffer extreme hardship if deported. You may apply even if you did not enter legally, and brief visits outside the United States which do not involve illegal activities will not break the continuity of your U.S. residence. The application is filed with an immigration judge on INS form 256A with the required fee.

Suspension of deportation is not available to persons who have failed to appear when required by the INS within the past five years, to persons who are in the United States as "J" exchange visitors, to foreign crew members, to persons who assisted in Nazi persecutions, or to persons who are applying to enter or re-enter the United States.

The first requirement for suspension of deportation is continuous residence in the United States for seven years, unless the reason you are being deported includes criminal offenses, failure to register, or falsification of documents, or grounds related to national security. If these apply to you, you must show an uninterrupted U.S. residence of ten years. If you are a ten year applicant, the period of residency which you must show is counted beginning at the date of the conviction, and thus persons with recent convictions will not be eligible to apply for suspension. You must show "good moral character" for the entire required period of residence.

Finally, if you are applying for suspension of deportation you must show that your forced departure from the United States would cause extreme hardship to you or your LPR or U.S. citizen spouse, child or parent. It is your responsibility to demonstrate "extreme" hardship. The immigration judge will decide whether the hardship to you or your family members is extreme. The factors the judge will consider include your age and health, and age and health of your spouse, children, or parents, the location of other family members, the conditions in the country of deportation, the degree to which you or your family members have integrated with the U.S. community, the number of years you have lived in the United States, and any other factors which the judge thinks are relevant to demonstrating hardship. Usually, economic hardship by itself is not enough to make this relief available.

The decision lies in the discretion of the judge, who will consider whether or not he thinks you deserve to remain in the United States. This is a complicated application and you should retain a competent and experienced immigration attorney. If your application for suspension of deportation is granted, your status is changed to that of lawful permanent resident, and you are a legal resident of the United States.

You must show that your forced departure from the United States would cause extreme hardship.

Registry

This route to permanent resident status was discussed in Chapter Two. An application for registry may also be made during a deportation hearing. The requirements will be the same. The immigration judge will make the decision.

Adjustment of Status

If you meet the requirements for adjustment of status to lawful permanent resident discussed in Chapter Three, the application can be filed with the immigration judge during the deportation hearing. If you meet the requirements and the judge grants your request, you will not be deported and will become a lawful permanent resident.

Waiver of Deportation

This way to avoid being deported is usually referred to as "212(c)" relief, as it is found in section 212(c) of the Immigration and Nationality Act. It originally applied only to permanent residents attempting to re-enter the United States, but it has found its way into the deportation process as a parallel waiver of certain reasons for deportation. It is the only means of preventing deportation available to persons convicted of certain drug offenses.

In order to be eligible for this waiver, you first must have seven years of unrelinquished lawful permanent residence. That means that you must have received your Alien Registration Card more than seven years earlier, and you must have resided in the United States during that time, except for short absences. In addition, the reason the INS is attempting to deport you must be the same as one of the reasons for which the INS could keep you from entering the country, listed in Chapter Three. This is a complicated area, but generally speaking, if you are being deported for entering illegally or for a firearms offense, the waiver will not be available. It is also not available if you have been convicted of an aggravated felony and have actually served a term of imprisonment of five years or more, if you are being deported for national security or foreign policy reasons, or if you have participated in genocide or terrorism.

You must convince the judge that you deserve to be allowed to remain in the United States.

The application is made on INS form I-191. You must show that you have been rehabilitated, and you must convince the judge that you deserve to be allowed to remain in the United States and that you will not again engage in the behavior that made it possible for the INS to try to deport you. This is a difficult application and you should be represented by an experienced immigration attorney.

Asylum and Withholding of Deportation

If you are eligible to be granted asylum, discussed in Chapter Two, you may file an application with the immigration judge in a deportation hearing. If it is granted, you will not be deported and you will be eligible in one year to apply for lawful permanent resident status.

Withholding of deportation is automatically considered by the immigration judge when you apply for asylum. Asylum and withholding of deportation are similar but not identical. If you meet the requirements for withholding of deportation, the judge must grant your application. The law states that any alien whose life or freedom would be threatened on account of any one or more of five categories: race, religion, nationality, membership in a particular social group, or political opinion may not be deported even if the alien is otherwise in the United States in violation of the law. The judge must find that the alien's life "would be threatened" in order to grant withholding. This is different from asylum, where the judge need only find that the alien has a "well-founded fear" of persecution due to one or more of the same five categories. However, a grant of asylum can result in permanent resident status one year later, while withholding results only in a stay of deportation until conditions in the alien's home country are such that it is safe to return.

A grant of asylum can result in permanent resident status one year later.

Any alien who has been convicted of a "particularly serious" crime, who has committed a serious nonpolitical crime outside the United States, who might reasonably be considered to be a danger to the United States, who can be deported because of association with a Nazi organization, or who has participated in any way in the persecution of others, is not eligible for withholding of deportation. There is no clear definition of "particularly serious" or "serious nonpolitical" crimes, but they certainly include drug offenses, violent crimes, and terrorist activities. The determination of whether a conviction or activity will bar a grant of withholding of deportation is left to the INS or the immigration judge.

Asylum will also not be granted in certain circumstances. An application for asylum must be denied if the alien has been convicted of a particularly serious crime in the United States, if the alien has been firmly resettled in another country prior to making application, or if there are reasonable grounds to regard him as a danger to the security of the United States.

An application for asylum must be denied if the alien has been convicted of a particularly serious crime in the U.S.

You can file an application for asylum with the INS even if you are in legal status and the INS is not trying to deport you. If your application for asylum is not frivolous, you must be given work authorization. Of course, when you file the application you are telling the INS that you are present in the United States, and that you want to stay permanently. This may not be wise if your application is weak and you are out of status or subject to being deported, as the INS may institute deportation proceedings now that it knows where you are. Proceedings will not be started, however, until the INS has decided whether it will grant or deny your application for asylum.

If the INS denies your application, you may refile it with the immigration judge in your deportation hearing as an application for relief from deportation. It will then automatically also be considered as an application for withholding of deportation. When filed during a deportation hearing, you will have the opportunity to present witnesses in support of your case, in addition to your own testimony and any documentary evidence that you may have, such as newspaper or magazine articles, reports on the political condition of your country by private sources such as Amnesty International, warrants for your arrest in your home country, threatening letters, and any other paper or testimony that tends to prove your claim of persecution or threatened persecution.

It is extremely important to appear for your hearing. If an alien who is out of status because he has stayed longer than authorized files an application for asylum and fails to appear for the hearing after having received proper notification, certain relief from being deported is no longer available. These persons will be ineligible for voluntary departure, suspension of deportation, and adjustment or change of status, unless they can show that there were exceptional circumstances excusing the nonappearance.

It is extremely important to appear for your deportation hearing.

Deferred Action

The district director of a local INS office has the authority to "defer," that is to not try to deport a particular person, if the district director believes there are appropriate reasons not to enforce the letter of the law. What constitutes an appropriate reason is not always clear, but compelling humanitarian concerns, administrative convenience, and the possibility of available relief to the alien in the future have justified deferred action in past cases. For example, the INS may allow a person to remain in the United States longer than usual to allow the person to obtain medical care. Or an elderly grandmother may be allowed to remain if there is no one to care for her in her native country. The power of the district director to decide whether or not to defer action in a particular matter is nearly absolute.

The power of the district director to decide whether to defer action is nearly absolute.

Private Legislation

In cases of extreme hardship where all other avenues have been unsuccessfully taken to prevent deportation, an alien may ask a U.S. Senator or Congressman to introduce special legislation allowing the alien to remain in the United States as a permanent resident. This is definitely a court of last resort and is rarely successful. Introduction of a private bill will not automatically stop the INS from actually carrying out the deportation unless a congressional subcommittee asks the INS for a report on the matter.

Deportation Hearings

Deportation hearings are conducted in an immigration court presided over by an immigration judge. They are civil trials which fall under the jurisdiction of the Executive Office of Immigration Review (EOIR), a sub-agency of the Department of Justice. EOIR contains the immigration courts and the Board of Immigration Appeals, which hears appeals of decisions rendered by immigration judges.

Proceedings begin with the service of an Order to Show Cause (OSC) on the alien by the INS, and the filing of the OSC with the court. The OSC must contain allegations of fact which, in the opinion of the INS, show sufficient cause for deportation, and it must specify the statutory provisions that the INS believes have been violated. The OSC also contains an important instruction: The alien must immediately notify the court and the INS in writing of his address and telephone number and report any future changes.

Deportation hearings are conducted in an immigration court presided over by an immigration judge.

If you do notify the court and the INS of a change in your address, future notices of the time and place of the hearing will be considered as received by you when sent to the last known address, even if you did not actually get them. The hearing can then proceed even though you are not present, and the judge may order that you be deported. Thus, it is extremely important that you comply with this instruction by keeping the INS informed of all address changes and any changes of attorney.

Immigration officers have the right to arrest and detain an alien if there is reason to believe that the alien is illegally present in the United States and may escape before a warrant can be obtained. The INS will usually set bond for a detained alien, but no bond is allowed for aggravated felons, unless they are LPRs. If the bond is too high, a detained alien may ask an immigration judge for a bond reduction hearing. The issues with respect to bond are whether the alien will be a threat to the community if he is released, and whether he is likely to appear at the hearing.

Eventually the court will set a time and place for your first appearance, known as a "master calendar" hearing. The purpose of this hearing is to allow you to agree or disagree with the allegations of fact in the OSC, so that the judge can determine whether a full hearing is necessary. If the only relief available can be decided at the first appearance, the matter may be concluded then. In some circumstances, the judge may postpone the master calendar hearing to allow you to get a lawyer, or to apply for expungement of a criminal conviction.

The master calendar appearance is important because the judge will inform you of your rights.

The master calendar appearance is also important because the judge will inform you of your rights. If you appear to be eligible for asylum, or suspension of deportation for example, the judge is required to inform you and allow you the opportunity to apply during the proceedings. You may request that the hearing be held elsewhere (called a Change of Venue) if your residence, witnesses, lawyer, etc. are elsewhere. Immigration judges play an active role in the deportation process and therefore can be very helpful to your understanding of your rights. Be sure to ask questions if you are at a hearing without a lawyer. Let the judge know if you need time to find a lawyer, or if you are confused by the process.

If you wish to show the judge that the INS claims in the OSC are not accurate or that you should not be deported because you can qualify for one of the remedies from deportation, a hearing on the merits of your claim will be set. You may be represented by an attorney, at your own expense. The Constitution of the United States requires the hearing process to be fair and reasonable. It must allow you the opportunity to present witnesses and documentation in support of your assertion that you are not in violation of immigration law, and therefore not subject to deportation. You have the right to cross-examine any witnesses presented by the INS. The court will provide an interpreter if necessary.

The INS will be represented by an attorney who must prove by clear and convincing evidence that your presence in the United States is in violation of the law, and that you are not deserving of any of the various kinds of relief from deportation. If the court rules against you, you may appeal its decision to the Board of Immigration Appeals, followed if necessary by a further appeal to one of the federal courts.

The deportation process should be treated with great respect. The consequences of a final order of deportation are severe, and the process is complex and difficult. It is wise to be represented by an attorney who is qualified to represent aliens in deportation proceedings.

The deportation process should be treated with great respect.

Consequences of Deportation

Included within the classes of persons who can be excluded from the United States are persons who have been ordered deported within five years of the date of application of admission (twenty tears if deported because of a conviction of an aggravated felony). Thus, a person who has been deported and removed from the United

States may not re-enter the country for either five or twenty years, depending on the reason for the deportation. The INS has the authority to consent to readmission before the statutory time period has passed, but the decision is wholly within the discretion of the INS, and such requests are not often granted.

CHAPTER SIX
NATURALIZATION: BECOMING A CITIZEN

Who Can Apply?

Only persons who are 18 years of age or older, who are lawfully admitted permanent resident aliens, and who meet the requirements discussed in this chapter, may apply to become naturalized citizens of the United States. Certain veterans of the armed forces of the United States are eligible for naturalization under a number of unusual provisions beyond the scope of this book. Aliens who have served in the U.S. military should contact the INS or their Senator or Congressman regarding the applicability of these unusual alternative naturalization provisions.

When Do You Apply?

You may apply five years from your date of entry as a lawful permanent resident. If you have been married to and living in marital union with a U.S. citizen for at least three years preceding the filing of the application for naturalization, the residence period is shortened to three years. If you have forgotten your entry date, it is on your Alien Registration Card. The application may be filed one month before you meet the residence requirements, but not until you have been a resident of the state or INS district where you are filing for naturalization for three months.

You may apply five years from your date of entry as a lawful permanent resident.

How Do You Apply?

Application for naturalization is made on INS form N-400 and filed with the district office of the INS where you reside. The waiting time varies from district to district, but eventually you will be mailed a notice of an examination date. At that interview, your application will be reviewed to ensure that the requirements of the law have been met, and you will be asked to answer 10 questions about U.S. government and history, and to demonstrate your proficiency in the English language by reading and writing a short sentence.

The INS has 120 days in which to grant or deny your application.

The INS then has 120 days in which to grant or deny your application, although usually it will be granted that day. You will then receive notice of the date you are to make the Oath of Allegiance, which at your choice may be held at the INS or at a U.S. district court. Immediately following the Oath of Allegiance ceremony, you will be given a certificate of citizenship.

If your application is denied, you may request review in a United States district court, which will review your application as though it had been newly filed.

Requirements For Naturalization

Each applicant for naturalization must satisfy four main requirements: 1) Basic literacy in the English language; 2) knowledge of U.S. history; 3) five years residency in the United States; and 4) good moral character.

Literacy in the English Language

The applicant must have an understanding of and literacy in the English language, which includes the ability to read and write simple words and phrases, and to understand ordinary usage.

The interview and examination are conducted in English, and you will be asked to read and write a simple sentence. For example, you may be asked to write "The horse jumped over the fence." The reading test is similarly simple. You will frequently find that the INS officers administering the tests are helpful and encouraging. Like everyone else, they are pleased to see new citizens, and often find naturalization interviews their favorite part of the job.

The interview and examination are conducted in English.

The English literacy requirement may be waived for persons who are otherwise qualified to naturalize, but are physically unable to comply, such as persons who are legally blind or hearing impaired. It also is waived for persons who are over the age of 50 and have been permanent residents of the United States for 20 years or more, or who are over 55 years of age and have lived in the United States for 15 years after entry for permanent residence.

Knowledge of History

The applicant must have a knowledge and understanding of the history, founding principles and form of government of the United States. The INS officer will conduct an oral examination of ten or twelve questions from a list of 100 questions which you may review in advance of the interview. This is not a difficult test, nor is it the desire of the examiner that you fail. The INS examiners will usually be very helpful and encouraging.

Residence Requirement

The applicant must have resided in the United States for at least five years after entry as a lawful permanent resident, and must have been physically present in the United States for at least half of that period, or for thirty months.

The residence and physical presence requirement for spouses of U.S. citizens is three years total after entry, and eighteen months of physical presence.

Absences from the United States of more than six months but less than one year will interrupt your continuous residence unless you can convince the INS that you did not in fact abandon your residence in the United States. Absence of one year or more will definitely break the continuity of your residence. If continuity of residence is broken, you must start the five year period over again in order to qualify for naturalization.

Exceptions to the residence requirement are sometimes made for certain employees of the U.S. government, U.S. research institutions and U.S. firms engaged in the development of international trade. To qualify, the employee must have one year of uninterrupted physical presence in the United States and prior approval of the INS. The request for approval is filed on INS form N-470.

There are also exceptions to the residence requirements for persons who are outside the

United States performing religious duties, for persons who are serving on certain U.S. vessels, and for LPR spouses of U.S. citizens who have been sent abroad by the U.S. government or a U.S. company engaged in international trade.

Moral Character

During the five or three year statutory residence period, the applicant must have been of good moral character. If you have been convicted of certain crimes, including drug offenses, fraud, theft, deliberate violence or money laundering, you will not be able to apply for naturalization until you have completed a new residence period in which you have demonstrated good moral character. In addition, persons who are habitual drunkards, professional gamblers, or practicing polygamists during the residency period are ineligible for naturalization.

Barriers to Naturalization

There are additional activities which may bar you from applying to become a U.S. citizen. The law forbids the naturalization of persons who advocate, or belong to any organization that advocates opposition to organized government. There may not be many organized anarchists left in the world today, but if there are, they are not eligible to become naturalized citizens of the United States.

Also barred from naturalization are members and affiliates of the Communist party of the United States or any individual state. Members of other communist or totalitarian organizations are similarly barred from naturalization, unless the member was not aware of the organization's

Persons who are habitual drunkards, professional gamblers, or practicing polygamists during the residency period are ineligible for naturalization.

nature. Finally, persons who openly advocate the overthrow of the U.S. government by force, violence, terrorism or sabotage, or who advocate such as writer or publisher, can be denied the opportunity for naturalized citizenship.

An alien who applied for exemption from service in the armed forces of the United States because of his alien status is barred from naturalization unless the exemption was pursuant to treaty rights, and the alien had already served in the armed forces of his own country.

Lastly, persons convicted of desertion from the military forces of the United States, or found guilty of draft evasion during wartime are permanently ineligible to naturalize.

The prohibitions listed above are not applicable if the activities took place more than ten years prior to filing the application for naturalization. They are also not applicable if you can demonstrate that your membership or activities were involuntary, were ended prior to your sixteenth birthday, were mandated by law, or were necessary in order to obtain employment, food rations or other essentials.

The Oath of Allegiance

Prior to being admitted to citizenship, all applicants must take the Oath of Allegiance by swearing:

> TO SUPPORT THE CONSTITUTION OF THE UNITED STATES; TO RENOUNCE AND ABJURE ABSOLUTELY AND ENTIRELY ALL ALLEGIANCE AND FIDELITY TO ANY FOREIGN PRINCE, POTENTATE, STATE, OR SOVEREIGNTY OF WHOM

OR WHICH THE APPLICANT WAS BEFORE A SUBJECT OR CITIZEN; TO SUPPORT AND DEFEND THE CONSTITUTION AND THE LAWS OF THE UNITED STATES AGAINST ALL ENEMIES, FOREIGN AND DOMESTIC; TO BEAR TRUE FAITH AND ALLEGIANCE TO THE SAME; AND TO BEAR ARMS ON BEHALF OF THE UNITED STATES WHEN REQUIRED BY LAW, OR TO PERFORM NONCOMBATANT SERVICE IN THE ARMED FORCES OF THE UNITED STATES WHEN REQUIRED BY THE LAW, OR TO PERFORM WORK OF NATIONAL IMPORTANCE UNDER CIVILIAN DIRECTION WHEN REQUIRED BY THE LAW.

The Oath may be modified if your religious training and beliefs do not allow you to affirm that you will bear arms or perform military service. For this purpose, religious training and beliefs do not include beliefs that are essentially political, sociological, philosophical or an expression of personal morality. You must demonstrate that your inability to take those portions of the Oath are due to your belief in a supreme being.

The Oath may be modified if your religious beliefs do not allow you to bear arms or perform military service.

Administration of the Oath of Allegiance is required to be performed in a dignified public ceremony. Ceremonies are held by the INS and by the U.S. district court.

Consequences of Citizenship

Citizens of the United States may apply for and travel under a U.S. passport, and receive the protection of the government when abroad. Citizens may vote, run for public office, and have the full rights and protection of the U.S. Constitution. Citizens may not be deported and may not be refused entry into the United States. Citizens may also petition for permanent resident status for their alien relatives—an important benefit.

Naturalized citizens may retain their citizenship status and the passport of their native country. There is no prohibition in U.S. law of dual nationality. If the new citizen's original country of citizenship has no law stating that obtaining U.S. citizenship acts as revocation of its nationality, a newly naturalized U.S. citizen may remain a citizen of both countries. However some countries, such as Japan and Germany, do not recognize simultaneous citizenship.

Naturalized citizens may retain their citizenship and the passport of their native country.

Denaturalization

Although there are a number of circumstances which can result in denaturalization, the Department of Justice policy is not to initiate denaturalization proceedings unless doing so would be of benefit to the nation. Thus, the most common situation in which the government attempts to revoke citizenship is where naturalization was obtained by willful misrepresentation of material facts. You may have heard of several recent cases involving former Nazis who concealed their wartime activities when applying for visas to enter the United States after World War II.

Although almost never seen, there are other situations in which the law provides that citizenship may be revoked. There is a presumption that a person was not attached to the principles of the Constitution and was not well disposed to the good order and happiness of the United States at the time of naturalization if certain behavior occurs after becoming a citizen. For example, if within ten years after naturalization, an individual refuses to testify before a congressional committee regarding alleged subversive activities, establishes a permanent foreign residence within five years, or becomes a member of a disallowed organization within five years, denaturalization proceedings may be instituted.

You cannot consider your U.S. citizenship to be permanent if any step along the way was procured by misrepresentation.

Denaturalization actions are not undertaken lightly by the Department of Justice, but it is well to remember that you cannot consider your U.S. citizenship to be permanent if any step along the way was procured by fraud or misrepresentation.

CONLUSION

As you have seen, the laws of the United States concerning immigration and naturalization are complicated. There are so many rules and regulations governing non-citizens that sometimes it is not easy to know how to get a friend or relative here just for a visit. But you can figure a lot of this out for yourself. Remember, you do not need to know every rule; just those that affect your situation.

If you need a lawyer's assistance, choose carefully. You may want to see if your lawyer is a member of the American Immigration Lawyers' Association (addresses and phone numbers are included in Appendix A), or is an active member of a local Bar Association for immigration lawyers. Ask your friends for recommendations, or check with ethnic organizations whose members may have had experience with immigration lawyers. Don't be afraid to visit with the lawyer first and ask questions, including the amount of fees and the experience the lawyer has had with cases like yours.

It is not always wise to rely upon the INS for answers to your questions. The "contact representatives" at the front counter of your local district office may not be well-trained, and it is not unusual to get incorrect advice from them. Even consular officers at U.S. Consulates abroad may be misinformed; usually they have such a heavy work load that it is impossible to speak to them long enough to explain your situation in detail. Your details are important, however, so any advice that you receive will be suspect unless the person giving

> *It is not always wise to rely upon the INS for answers to your questions.*

the advice knows everything about your particular situation.

Finally, do not take the immigration process lightly. Always be truthful and candid when answering questions or filling out forms. Do not be tempted to short-cut the process by involving yourself in a fraudulent scheme. Do not try to avoid the system, but instead find out how to work with the system and to make it work for you.

Good luck!

APPENDIX A

INS Address List

DEPARTMENT OF STATE

Public Inquiries Division

2401 E Street, NW

Washington, DC 20522-0113

(202) 663-1254

AMERICAN IMMIGRATION LAWYERS ASS'N.

1400 Eye Street, NW, Suite 1200

Washington, DC 20005

(202) 371-9377

INS REGIONAL OFFICES

EASTERN:	SOUTHERN:
Federal Building	P.O. Box 568808
Elmwood Avenue	7701 Stemmons Freeway
Burlington, VT 05401	Dallas, TX 75356-8808
(802) 951-6201/6223	(214) 767-7012

NORTHERN:	WESTERN:
Bishop Henry Whipple Federal Building	P.O. Box 30080 24000 Avila Road
Room 401; Fort Snelling	Laguna Niguel, CA 92677
Twin Cities, MN 55111	(714) 643-6118
(612) 725-4450/3850/3855/3470	Fax: (714) 643-4808

LOCAL INS OFFICES

Anchorage District
620 E. 10th Avenue
Room #102
Anchorage, Alaska 99501
(907) 343-7820

    Fairbanks Suboffice
    P.O. Box 60208
    Fairbanks, Alaska 99706
    (907) 474-0307
    (Accepts paper for filing only)

Chicago District
Dirksen Federal Office Building
219 S. Dearborn Street
Chicago, Illinois 60604
(312) 353-7334

    Indiana Suboffice
    46 E. Ohio Street
    Room #124
    Indianapolis, Indiana 46204
    (317) 225-6009

    Wisconsin Suboffice
    Federal Building
    Room #186
    517 E. Wisconsin Avenue
    Milwaukee, Wisconsin 53202
    (414) 297-3565

Cleveland District
Anthony Celebrezze Federal Bldg.
Room 1917
1240 E. 9th Street
Cleveland, Ohio 44199
(216) 522-4770

    Cincinnati Suboffice
    J.W. Peck Federal Building
    550 Main Street
    Room #8525
    Cincinnati, Ohio
    (513) 684-6080

Denver District
Albrecht Center
4730 Paris Street
Denver, Colorado 80239
(303) 371-3041

    Utah Suboffice
    230 W. 400 South Street
    Salt Lake City, Utah 84101
    (801) 524-5771/5772

Detroit District
150 E. Jefferson
Detroit, Michigan 48226
(313) 226-3290

Helena District
Federal Building
Room #512
301 South Park, Drawer 10036
Helena, Montana 59626
(406) 449-5288

    Idaho Suboffice
    4620 Overland Road
    Room #108
    Boise, Idaho 83705
    (208) 334-1821

Kansas City District
9747 North Conant Avenue
Kansas City, Missouri 63103
(816) 891-0603

    St. Louis Suboffice
    1222 Spruce Street
    St. Louis Missouri 63103
    (314) 539-2532

Omaha District
3736 South 132nd Street
Omaha, Nebraska 68144
(402) 697-9155

Portland District
Federal Office Building
511 N.W. Broadway
Portland, Oregon 97209
(503) 325-3006

St. Paul District
2901 Metro Drive
Bloomington, Minnesota 55101
(612) 854-7754

Seattle District
Immigration Building
815 Airport Way, South
Seattle, Washington 98134
(206) 553-5956

> **Spokane Suboffice**
> 691 Federal Courthouse Bldg.
> W. 920 Riverside
> Spokane, Washington 99201
> (509) 353-2129

Baltimore District
E.A. Garmatz Federal Building
101 W. Lombard Street
Room #1100
Baltimore, Maryland 21201
(301) 962-2120

Boston District
John F. Kennedy Federal Bldg.
Room #E-132
Government Center
Boston, Massachusetts 02203
(617) 565-3879

> **Connecticut Suboffice**
> Abraham Ribicoff Federal Bldg
> Room #410
> 450 Main Street
> Hartford, Connecticut 06103
> (203) 240-3171

Rhode Island Suboffice
Pastore Federal Building
Room #203
Kennedy Plaza
U.S. Post Office
Providence, RI 02903
(401) 454-7440

Buffalo District
68 Court Street
Room #113
Buffalo, New York 14202
(716) 849-6760

> **Albany Suboffice**
> James T. Foley
>   Federal Courthouse
> Room #227
> 445 Broadway
> Albany, New York 12207
> (518) 472-4621

Newark District
Federal Building
970 Broad Street
Room #136
Newark, New Jersey 07102
(201) 645-4400

New York District
Jacob Javits Federal Building
26 Federal Plaza
New York, New York 10278
(212) 206-6500

Philadelphia District
1600 Callowhill Street
Philadelphia, Pennsylvania 19103
(215) 597-3961

LOCAL INS OFFICES, (continued)

Pittsburgh Suboffice
2130 Federal Building
1000 Liberty Avenue
Pittsburgh, PA 15222
(412) 644-3356

Portland District
739 Warren Avenue
Portland, Maine 04103
(207) 780-3352

Vermont Suboffice
Federal Building
50 South Main Street
P.O. Box 328
St. Albans, Vermont 05478
(802) 951-6658

San Juan District
Federal Building
Room #380
Chardon Street
Hato Rey, Puerto Rico 00935
(809) 766-5280

St. Croix Suboffice
P.O. Box 1270
Kingshill
Christian Sted.
St. Croix, Virgin Islands 00850
(809) 778-6559

St. Thomas Suboffice
Federal Building
Veterans Drive
P.O. Box 610
Charlotte Amalie
St. Thomas, V.I. 00804
(809) 774-1390

Washington D.C. District
Arlington Financial Building
4420 North Fairfax Drive
Room #210
Arlington, Virginia 22203
(703) 235-4055

Virginia Suboffice
Norfolk Federal Building
200 Granby Mall
Room #439
Norfolk, Virginia 23510
(804) 441-3081

Atlanta District
Dr. Martin Luther King, Jr.
Federal Building
77 Forsythe Street, S.W.
Atlanta, Georgia 30303
(404) 331-5158

North Carolina Suboffice
6 Woodlawn Green
Room #138
Charlotte, NC 28217
(704) 523-1704

South Carolina Suboffice
Federal Building
Room #110
334 Meeting Street
Charleston, SC 29403
(803) 724-4350

Dallas District
8101 N. Stemmons Highway
Dallas, Texas 75247
(214) 655-5384

Oklahoma Suboffice
4149 Highline Blvd., Suite 300
Oklahoma City, OK 73108
(405) 942-8670

El Paso District
700 East San Antonio
P.O. Box 9398
El Paso, Texas 79984
(915) 534-6366

> **New Mexico Suboffice**
> 517 Gold Avenue SW
> Room #1010
> Albuquerque, NM 87103
> (505) 766-2378

Harlingen District
2102 Teege Avenue
Harlingen, Texas 78550
(512) 425-7333

Houston District
509 North Belt (Main Floor)
Houston, Texas 77060
(713) 847-7900

Miami District
7880 Biscayne Road
Room #100
Miami, Florida 33138
(305) 536-5741

> **Jacksonville Suboffice**
> 400 West Bay Street
> Room G-18
> PO. Box 35039
> Jacksonville, Florida 32202
> (904) 791-2625

> **Tampa Suboffice**
> 5509 West Gray Street
> Room #113
> Tampa, Florida 33609
> (813) 228-2131

Riviera Beach Suboffice
4 East Port Road
Room #129
P.O. Box 9846
Riviera Beach, Florida 33404
(407) 844-4341

New Orleans District
Postal Service Building
Room #8011
701 Loyola Avenue
New Orleans, Louisiana 70113
(504) 589-6533

> **Kentucky Suboffice**
> U.S. Courthouse Building
> Room #601
> West 6th & Broadway
> Louisville, Kentucky 40202
> (502) 582-6375

> **Tennessee Suboffice**
> 245 Wagner Place
> Room #250
> Memphis, Tennessee 38103
> (901) 544-3301

San Antonio District
U.S. Federal Building
Room #19
727 E. Durango
San Antonio, Texas 78206
(512) 229-6350

Honolulu District
595 Ala Moana Boulevard
Honolulu, Hawaii 96813
(808) 541-1379

LOCAL INS OFFICES, (continued)

Guam Suboffice
801 Pacific News Building
238 O'Hara Street
Agana, Guam 96910
(671) 472-7349

Los Angeles District
Federal Building
300 North Los Angeles Street
Room #1001
Los Angeles, California 90012
(213) 894-2119

Phoenix District
2035 North Central Avenue
Phoenix, Arizona 85004
(602) 379-3122

    Tucson Suboffice
    Federal Building
    300 West Congress
    Room #1-T
    Tucson, Arizona 85701
    (602) 670-6229

    Las Vegas Suboffice
    Foley Federal Building
    Room #104
    300 Las Vegas Blvd., South
    Las Vegas, Nevada 89101
    (702) 384-3696

    Reno Suboffice
    712 Mill Street
    Reno, Nevada 89502
    (702) 784-5427

San Diego District
U.S. Federal Building
880 Front Street
Room #1-F13
San Diego, California 92188
(619) 557-5570

San Francisco District
Appraisers Building
Room #200
630 Sansome Street
San Francisco, California 94111
(415) 705-4411

    Fresno Suboffice
    Federal Building
    Room #1308
    1130 "O" Street
    Fresno, California 93721
    (209) 487-5091

    Sacramento Suboffice
    711 Jay Street
    Sacramento, California 95814
    (916) 551-2785

    San Jose Suboffice
    Federal Building & Courthouse
    Room #1150
    280 South First Street
    San Jose, California 95113
    (408) 291-7876

APPENDIX B

Acquisition of Citizenship Charts[*]

* Three charts reprinted from Robert A. Mautino, "Acquisition of Citizenship," 90-4 Immigration Briefings pages 5-7 (April 1990). Copyright © 1990 by Federal Publications Inc. Reprinted with permission of Immigration Briefings.

CHART 1
BIRTH OUTSIDE U.S. TO CITIZEN PARENT(S)—LEGITIMATE BIRTHS

DATE OF BIRTH OF CHILD	RESIDENCE REQUIRED OF PARENT(S) TO TRANSMIT CITIZENSHIP	RESIDENCE REQUIRED OF CHILD TO RETAIN CITIZENSHIP
Before 5/24/34	Father is citizen who resided in U.S. before birth. One court has held mothers transmit as well.	None
On or after 5/24/34 and before 1/13/41	Both parents are citizens, one with prior residence.	None
	One parent is citizen with prior residence.	Same as immediately below
On or after 1/13/41 and before 12/24/52	One parent is citizen with 10 years of prior residence in the U.S., at least 5 of which were after age 16. (If citizen parent had honorable military service between 12/7/41 and 12/31/46, sufficient if the 5 years were after age 12. If military service was between 12/31/46 and 12/24/52, parent needs 10 years physical presence, at least 5 of which are after age 14.)	Two years continuous presence in the U.S. between ages 14-28, except no retention requirement if born on or after 10/10/52. (Exception: No retention requirements if citizen parent was employed by certain U.S. organizations at time of birth. This exception does not apply if citizenship is transmitted under military service exemptions in box to the left.
	Both parents are citizens, one with prior residence in U.S.	None
On or after 12/24/52	Both parents are citizens, one with prior residence in U.S.	None
	One citizen parent with 10 years of prior physical presence in the U.S., at least 5 of which were after age 14 (for births 12/24/52 to 11/13/86) OR One citizen parent with 5 years of prior physical presence in the U.S., at least 2 of which were after age 14(for births on or after 11/14/86)	None. The retention requirement was abolished effective 10/10/78. Persons still eligible on that date have no retention requirements. Persons who lost citizenship through failure to satisfy previous retention requirements may not be reinstated.

CHART 2
BIRTH OUTSIDE U.S. TO CITIZEN PARENT(S)—ILLEGITIMATE BIRTHS

CHILD NOT LEGITIMATED	
Date of Birth of Child	**Requirements for Transmission of Citizenship**
Before 12/24/52	Mother was a U.S. citizen who had resided in the U.S. or its outlying possessions before birth of child. A child born before 5/24/34 acquired U.S. citizenship when the Nationality Act of 1940 bestowed citizenship retroactive to date of birth.
On or after 12/24/52	Mother was a U.S. citizen who had been physically present in the U.S. or its outlying possessions for a continuous period of 1 year before birth of child.

CHILD LEGITIMATED BY ALIEN FATHER

The general rule is that citizenship acquired by an illegitimate child through its citizen mother is not affected by later legitimation by an alien father. The only exception is that citizenship is not transmitted by a U.S. citizen mother if an illegitimate child is legitimated by an alien father and all three of these conditions are met: 1) Child was born before 5/24/34; 2) child was legitimated before age 21; and 3) the legitimation was before 1/13/41.

CHILD LEGITIMATED BY U.S. CITIZEN FATHER

Legitimation makes a child legitimate at birth. Therefore, the transmission and retention requirements applicable to legitimate children born outside the U.S. (chart 1) apply. In other words, if the child did not acquire citizenship through its mother, but was legitimated by a U.S. citizen father under the following conditions, apply the appropriate provisions of Chart 1. No legitimation at all is required for children of certain veterans of World War II.

Date of Birth of Child: Before 1/13/41	1. Child legitimated at any time after birth under law of father's domicile. 2. Father had the required residence at time of child's birth. 3. No residence required for child to retain U.S. citizenship.
On or after 1/13/41 and before 12/24/52	1. Child legitimated before age 21 under law of father's domicile. 2. Father had the required residence at time of child's birth. 3. Child complies with residence requirements for retention.
On or after 12/24/52	1. Child legitimated before age 21 under law of father's domicile. 2. Father had the required residence at time of child's birth. 3. Child must be unmarried.

CHILD LEGITIMATED OR ACKNOWLEDGED BY U.S. CITIZEN FATHER

Child born on or after 11/15/68, and relationship established on or after 11/14/86	1. Child/father blood relationship established. 2. Father, unless deceased, must provide written statement under oath that he will provide financial support for child until child reaches 18. 3. Child must be legitimated under law of child's residence or domicile, or father must acknowledge paternity of child in writing under oath, or paternity must be established by competent court. 4. Father must have been a U.S. citizen and met the required residence requirement at time of child's birth. 5. Child must be under 18 when legitimated or acknowledged. (Child of age 15-18 on 11/14/86 may elect to acquire citizenship under prior law.)

CHART 3
DERIVATIVE CITIZENSHIP OF CHILD
THROUGH NATURALIZATION OF PARENT

Period in which last condition was fulfilled	Age of child before which conditions must be fulfilled	Conditions		Qualifications
		Immigration status of child (all periods)	Naturalization of parents	
Before 5/24/34	21	Lawful admission to U.S. for permanent residence	Either Parent	None
On or after 5/24/34 and before 1/13/41	21	Same as above	Either Parent	U.S. citizenship began 5 years after child began to reside in U.S. permanently.
	21	Same as above	Both Parents	None
On or after 1/13/41 and before 12/24/52	18	Same as above	Both Parents	Illegitimate child did not derive in this period (but see text below).
On or after 12/24/52 and before 10/5/78	16	Same as above	Both Parents	Marriage of child bars derivation in this period.
On or after 10/5/78 (see page 4)	18	Same as above	Both Parents	
On or after 11/14/86 (see page 4)	18	Same as above	Both Parents	

Index

A

"A" number (see Alien registration number)
Abandonment, 54-57 (see also unabandoned foreign residence)
Acquisition of Citizenship charts, 99-102
Afghanistan, 60
Africa, 34
Alien
  arrest of, 75-76
  definition, 2, 9
  principal, 13
  relative, 22-24, 27
  rights and restrictions, 53
  spouse, 24-26
  stateless, 60
  types, 3
Alien Registration Card, 22, 23, 46, 53, 57, 70, 79
Alien registration number, 53
American Immigration Lawyers' Association, 88, 92
Amnesty, 37
Amnesty International, 73
Ancestors, 8
Application for Adjustment of Status, 24 (see also Family-sponsored immigrant visas)

Asylum
  applying for, 73, 76
  restrictions, 72
  status, 33-35, 71
  status of immediate family, 35

B

Bar Association, 88
Birth certificate, 7
Board of Immigration Appeals, 57, 75-76

C

Canada,
  eligibility of medical schools, 18
  port of entry to U.S., 21
  status of citizens, 21
Certificate of Citizenship, 7, 80
Change of venue, 76
China, 60
Citizenship
  by marriage, 6-7
  eligibility, 4
  demonstrating a claim, 5
  derivative claims, 4, 7
  loss of, 8
  of adopted children, 6
  of illegitimate children, 5
  proving, 7

residency requirements, 4-6
retention requirements, 5
rights, 58, 60, 85-86
veterans, 6
Clinton administration, 40
Code of Federal Regulations, 1
Communist party, 83
Comprehensive Crime
Control Act, 65
Conditional Permanent
Residence Status, 25, 33, 61
Congressional committee, 87
Congressman, 79
Consulate's Treaty Visa
Questionnaire, 14 (see also
Non-immigrant visas,
"E-2" treaty investor)

D

Deferred inspection, 55-56
(see also Permanent
resident, loss of status)
Deportation
application for waiver, 42-
43, 48, 62, 70-71
changes to reasons for, 64
deferred action, 73-74
denial of request for entry, 46
for being out of status, 49,
51, 57-58, 72-73
final order of exclusion, 58
grounds, 40-42, 58, 61-63
hearing, 66, 69, 71, 73-76
laws, 60
postponement of
proceedings, 65
private legislation, 74

proceedings, 59-60, 72
request for relief from, 34,
64, 73
request for withholding of,
34, 71-73
suspension of, 67-68, 73, 76
temporary exceptions, 60
voluntary departure, 66-67, 73
Diplomats
children of, 4
status of, 4
Diversity transition visa, 35
(see also Miscellaneous visas)
Diversity visa, 36 (see also
Miscellaneous visas)

E

Educational Commission of
Foreign Medical
Graduates (ECFMG), 19
El Salvador, 60
Employment-based
immigrant visas
1A: extraordinary ability, 29
1B: outstanding professors
and researchers, 29-30
1C: multinational
executives and managers, 30
2A: advanced degrees, 30
2B: exceptional ability, 30-31
3A: professionals, 31
3B: skilled workers, 31
3C: other workers, 31-32
first preference (priority
workers), 29-30
fifth preference, investors,
32-33

fourth preference:
  ministers and religious
  workers, 32
second preference, 30-31
third preference, 31-32
Employment Authorization
  Document (EAD), 50-51
Employment creation visa,
  13, 32 (see also Non-
  immigrant visas, "E-2"
  treaty investor)
Entering Without Inspection
  (EWI), 61 (see also
  Deportation, grounds for
  excludability)
Entry to U.S., 43-51, 56
Excludibility (see Deportation,
  grounds for)
Exclusion, 2, 57-58 (see also
  Deportation)
Exclusion hearing, 56-58
  (see also Deportation)
Executive Office of Immigra-
  tion Review (EOIR), 74-75
Expatriating acts, 8, 9 (see
  Citizenship, loss of)
Expungement, 64-66 (see
  Deportation)

F

Family-sponsored
immigrant visas
  first preference: un-
  married sons or daugh-
  ters of U.S. citizens, 27
  fourth preference:
  brothers and sisters of
  U.S. citizens, 28

immediate relatives:
  spouse, parents and
  children of U.S. citizens,
  23-27
second preference A:
  spouses and minor
  children of permanent
  residents, 27
second preference B: adult
  unmarried sons and
  daughters of permanent
  residents, 28
third preference: married
  sons and daughters of
  U.S. citizens, 28
Federation of State Medical
  Boards (FLEX) exam, 18
Foreign Agents Registration
  Act, 63
Forms
  DOL form, ETA 750A
  DOL form, ETA 750B
  INS form I-20AB, 15
  INS form I-20ID, 15
  INS form I-20MN, 21
  INS form I-94, 15, 48
  INS form I-129, 16-18, 20-21, 22
  INS form I-129F, 19
  INS form I-130, 23, 27
  INS form I-140, 28, 30-31, 37
  INS form I-191, 70
  INS form I-256A, 68
  INS form I-360, 32
  INS form N-400, 80
  INS form N-470, 82
  INS form I-485, 24, 38
  INS form I-526, 33

INS form I-589, 35
INS form N-600, 7
INS form I-601, 42
INS form I-751, 25-26
INS form I-765, 51
State Department form
DSP-11, 7
State Department form
OF-156, 11-12, 14, 18, 44
Supplement H, 16-18
Supplement L, 20-21
Supplement R, 22
France, 10

G

Germany, 10, 86
Governor, 65
Green card, 3, 22, 52, 59 (see
Alien Registration Card)
"Green Card" (motion
picture), 26
Guam, 4

H

Health Care Facility
Attestation, 16 (see also
Non-immigrant visas,
"H1-A" registered nurse)
Hong Kong, 36
Hong Kong provisions, 36
Hungary, 34

I

Immigrant (see Permanent
resident)

Immigrated alien (see
Permanent resident)
Immigrant investor visa, 13,
53, 61 (see also Non-
immigrant visas, "E-2"
treaty investor)
Immigration
attorney, 19, 38, 46, 61,
69, 71, 76, 88
inspector, 46, 55
judge, 34, 46, 56-59, 64-76
reasons for, 2
regulations, 1
U.S. law, 2, 11, 49, 57, 65
Immigration and Nationality
Act, 1, 70
Immigration and Naturalization Service, (INS), 1, 7, 10
15, 16, 19, 23-27, 40-42,
46-49, 51-59, 63-66,
70-74, 77-83, 88
Income tax, 49
India, 35
INS offices, 16-17, 21-23,
27-28, 33, 38, 79-80, 92-97
Italy, 10

J

J exchange visitors, 68
Japan, 86
Joint Petition to Remove the
Conditional Basis of
Alien's Permanent Resi-
dence Status, 25 (see
also Family-sponsored
immigrant visas)

L

Labor Certification, 29, 37
(see also Employment-
based immigrant visas)
Labor Condition Attestation
(LCA), 17 (see also Non-
immigrant visa, H1-B,
specialty occupation)
Lawful permanent resident
(LPR) (see permanent
resident)
Lebanon, 60
Liberia, 60
Lottery visa, 36 (see also
Miscellaneous visas)

M

Marginality, 14 (see also
Non-immigrant visas,
"E-2" treaty investor)
Marriage to alien
anti-fraud rules, 25-26, 59, 61
ending a marriage, 26
proof of hardship or abuse, 6
proving "good faith," 25-26
requirements, 20
Master calendar hearing, 76
Mexico, 27
Military Selective Service
Act, 63
Miscellaneous visas
displaced Tibetans, 35
diversity and transitional
programs, 35
registry, 37-39
schedule A, 37
widows/widowers, 39

Moral turpitude, 62, 64 (see
also Deportation, grounds
for excludibility)

N

National, 12, 13
Naturalization,
application, 53, 79-83
barriers to, 83-84
ceremony, 85
denaturalization, 86-87
dual nationality, 86
examination, 80-82
oath of allegiance, 80, 84-85
residence requirements, 79
rights, 58, 85-86
veterans, 79
waiting period, 80
Nazi persecutions, 41, 63,
68, 71, 86
Nepal, 35
Non-immigrant visas
B temporary visitor, for
business or tourism, 11, 16
E-1 treaty trader, 12, 13
E-2 treaty investor, 13, 14
F-1 academic student, 14-16
H-1A registered nurse, 16
H-1B specialty occupation,
16-18
H-3 trainee, 18
J-1 exchange visitor, 19
K fiancee of U.S. citizen, 19
L-1 intracompany
transferee, 0-21
M-1 non-academic student, 1
R-1 religious worker, 22

Northern Mariana Islands, 4

O

Oath of allegiance, 8, 80
Order of Expungement, 65
Order to Show Cause
   (OSC), 75-76

P

Pardon (see also Deportation)
   foreign, 65
   presidential, 65
Parole, 55 (see also Permanent resident, loss of status)
Passport, 4, 7, 8, 10, 46, 52, 85
Permanent resident
   definition of, 3
   loss of status, 54-59
   registry, 69
   residence, 52, 59, 63, 70, 75
   restrictions, 54
   rights, 56
   status, 7, 20, 42, 52, 59, 71, 74
Petition for Alien Fiancee,
   19 (see also Non-immigrant
   visa, K fiancee of U.S.
   citizen)
Petition to Employ
   Intracompany Transferee,
   20-21 (see also Non-immigrant visas, L-1 Intracompany transferee)
Petition to Employ
   Temporary Worker or
   Trainee, 17 (see also
   Non-immigrant status,
   H1-B, specialty occupation)

Petition for Prospective
   Immigrant Employee, 28
   (see also Employment-
   based Immigrant visas)
Philippines, 27
Poland, 60
Port of entry, 46-47, 55 (see
   also Entry to U.S.)
President, 34, 60
Private legislation, 74 (see
   also Deportation)
Puerto Rico, 4

R

Refugees,
   status, 33-34
Relative petition, 23 (see
   also Family-sponsored
   immigrant visas)
Rescission of status, 58-59
Resident alien (see also
   Permanent resident)

S

Secretary of State, 64
Senator, 74, 79
Somalia, 60
Soviet Union, 34

T

212(c) relief, 70 (see
   Deportation, see applying
   for waiver)
Tax resident, 49

Trading With the Enemy
Act, 63
Treason, 9
Treaty alien, 12 (see also
Non-immigrant visas,
"E-1" treaty trader)
Treaty country, 12, 13 (see
also Non-immigrant visas,
"E-1" treaty trader)
Treaty investor, 13, 14 (see
also Non-immigrant visas,
"E-2" treaty investor)

U

Unabandoned foreign
residence, 15. 46, 54
United Kingdom, 10
United Nations High
Commissioner for
Refugees, 34
United States Code, 1
United States Congress, 2,
16, 22, 33-35, 40, 60-61, 63
United States Constitution,
1, 2, 4, 45, 52-54, 56, 76,
85-86
United States Consulate
office, 10-14, 17-21, 23-24,
40-45, 47-48, 52, 88
registration, 7
officer of, 9, 11, 14-16, 44-45
United States Department of
Health/Human Services, 40
United States Department of
Justice, 10, 75, 86-87
United States Department of
Labor (DOL), 16-17, 29, 32, 37

United States Department of
State, 7, 10, 34, 36, 42, 44,
47, 51, 61, 92
United States District Court,
80, 85
United States Government
Printing Office, 2
United States Information
Agency (USIA), 19
United States Social Security
Administration, 50

V

Vietnam, 34
Virgin Islands, 4
Visa
appealing a denial, 47
adjustment of status, 24,
27, 39, 44, 47-48, 59, 69, 73
change of status, 15-16,
47, 69, 73
countries that waive
requirement, 10
Duration of Status (D/S)
stamp, 15
extension of status, 13, 18, 48
fraud, 27, 89
immigrant status, 22-35, 45-48
non-immigrant status,
10-22, 44-45, 47
miscellaneous categories,
35-39
quotas, 18, 22, 35-36
reapplying, 44-45
status of Canadian
students, 21

status of Canadian
   medical schools, 18
temporary, 3
terms, 50
tourist, 10
waiving requirements, 32, 46
Voluntary return (see
   Deportation, voluntary
      departure)

W

Washington, D.C., 36
Work authorization
   document, 52, 72 (see also
      Employment Authoriza-
      tion Document (EAD)
Writ of audita querela, 66
Writ of error coram nobis, 66
Writ of habeas corpus, 66